Getting Ready
to Get a Job
in the 21ˢᵗ Century.

Bruce Bendinger
& The Copy Workshop

BRAND YOU!
Getting Ready to Get a Job in the 21st Century.

©2017 Bruce Bendinger

ISBN# 978-1-887229-48-7

DISCLAIMER: There are few guarantees in life. That includes career advice. What is true in general may or may not be right for an individual. The advice and recommendations in this book are based on proven principles and success in the marketplace. That said, in a changing world, you still need to develop your own best judgment based on your personal evaluations of circumstance and opportunity. If your judgment is good, you will know – because you are successful. If you are unsuccessful, you've already learned something – you might need to develop better judgment – and work harder. End of disclaimer.

Published by **The Copy Workshop**

A division of Bruce Bendinger Creative Communications, Inc.

2144 N. Hudson • Chicago, IL 60614

773-871-1179 FX: 773-281-4643

www.adbuzz.com • thecopyworkshop@aol.com

To: J. Roy Sandstrom,
Executive Art Director extraordinaire.

You showed me
how everything could be done
with taste, clarity, and faith.

(I know, I should have set this in Souvenir.)

BRAND YOU!
Getting Ready to Get a Job in the 21st Century.
by Bruce Bendinger

Table of Contents:

Design is not just what it looks
and feels like. Design is how it works.

Steve Jobs

www.thequotes.in

5

Introduction to the Introduction.

THANK YOU, LEWIS PERLSON. Back when I was your age – give or take – and getting ready for my university education, my father gave me some career advice.

"Son," he said (he called me that), *"I think that someone with a law degree and a degree in accounting will probably do very well in this world."*

He was right. It was good advice. Very good advice.

Only, as I discovered during my first two weeks of Accounting 101, it just wasn't advice for me.

This was early in my college career. Good thing. Suddenly, I was faced with a life-changing challenge.

I had to figure out what I was going to do for a living – and even though there were a lot of things I did not know, I was absolutely certain that it wasn't going to be accounting!

Years later, at a high school reunion, I saw that a smart classmate, Lewis Perlson, had built himself a nice life and a nice career with degrees in law and accounting.

I went over and thanked him for taking my place.

He seemed slightly surprised.

As for me, I was deeply grateful. Thanks again, Lew.

Courtesy Whitefish Bay High School Yearbook.

Bruce.   Lewis.

Introduction.

Introduction.

READ THIS. With some books, you can sort of skip the Introduction and move ahead quickly to Chapter One. Not this book.

With each section we're going to start by giving you an idea of what we want you to get from each section. At the end of each chapter, we'll take a bit of time to list some Things To Do – or maybe just some things to think about and Discuss.

The Purpose of This Book.

Our goal is to help you get on the road to getting the kind of job you want – even if you don't know what that is yet.

As you work to prepare, there are a lot of things you can do – whatever that job is. Better yet, you can do a lot of it without knowing where you'll end up.

At the center of it all is you building your brand – or as we describe it, "Brand You!" Got it?

Here's what we want you to start thinking about:

* **What are your "going-in premises?"** What's the "good advice" that you're currently working with?

    What is your random collection of hypotheses, best guesses, attractive examples and vaguely-remembered inspirational speeches, magazine articles, and pamphlets from the career counselor's office?

    You've collected a lot of information. What is it? Does it apply to you and your situation? Take a harder look.

* **What are your "prospects?"** We're guessing that neither the major league scout nor the NBA agent have been calling.

    So... wherever you're going, what resources and connections do you have that are going to help you get there?

    The good news – you already have more than you think.

Building your connections and career data base is just one of the tasks we'll be working on. In Chicago, we have a saying, *"Don't send nobody nobody sent."* Hold that thought.

- **Are you ready to "get serious?"** The sooner you do, the better. In school, the consequences can sometimes be serious – but they're usually, not fatal.

    In the real world, a missed deadline, not doing all that was asked, or any of quite a few things, can be career-threatening – or terminating. Want to make a living in a challenging world? Good. Take it seriously.

- **Remember, you are in charge of you.** You've got a job to do, and the person you're working for is... you. Let's help that person succeed.

Things To Do:

At the end of each of these sections, we'll have some things for you to do. Sometimes they are actual actions – things you have to do. Sometimes it's just a "quick think."

That's right, we just want you to sit and think about it.
This is one of those.
So... how about a quick review? A "quick think."

- **What are your "going-in premises?"** What kind of career are you preparing for? Where did this decision come from? What information helped you make that decision?

- **What are your "prospects?"** Well? Is it all worked out, with a job waiting for you in the family firm? Or are we talking hopes and dreams? Nothing wrong with that, but you probably need to start gathering a lot information.

- **Are you ready to "get serious?"** Is this just something you say to inquiring relatives, or are you committed to really making it happen? And, are you pretty sure that this is something you really want to do day after day after day?

Yes would be a good answer. But you might still need time to think about it. A slow think, maybe.

- **Remember, you are in charge of you.** Who are you doing this for? Sure, you want friends and family to be proud of you. But what about you? More thinking.

You don't have to answer all these questions right now, and you don't have to know everything. But these are some of the issues you should be facing up to. Bet you know that.

So...
Sit back. Deep breath. Give it some thought.
Want to write a few notes? Good idea. Do that.
Ready? Let's go. Next page. Chapter One.

1. How to Get Where You Want to Go
(When You Still Don't Know Exactly Where You're Going.)

THAT'S THE PROBLEM, ISN'T IT? At this stage, for most of us, it's really hard to know. Better yet, even if we think we have a pretty good idea of where our not-yet-career is headed, there's a pretty good chance we've got some of it wrong.

So, for a start, let's look at a few things we know – as opposed to all those things we don't know.

Welcome to the Revolution.

We can be quite certain that, here in the 21st Century, there are two kinds of revolutionary changes going on.

- **Revolutionary Change #1.** Let's call this The 21st Century Marketplace.

- **Revolutionary Change #2.** This is what we'll call The New Normal. They're related – but slightly different.

Let's take them one at a time.

Revolutionary Change #1: The 21st Century Marketplace.

Companies and business models that have been around doing successful business for 100 years are suddenly disappearing.

New business models are emerging. Suddenly.

Meanwhile, the speed of change is accelerating.

That means information that might have made sense five or ten years ago might already be old news.

Or is it? Hard to tell, isn't it?

Time for a story. Once upon a time, a new technology emerged – the automobile.

From replacement to reorganization.

At first, the car just kind of replaced the horse.

Then, society *reorganized* around this new technology. Roads got better. Trucks added a new level to our distribution system. People could move to new homes in the suburbs and drive to work.

Business models changed. The competition for your downtown store wasn't another store down the street – it was a shopping mall or supermarket surrounded by lots of parking in a brand new subdivision. Old business models had to change.

It was gradual, but by the middle of the 20th Century, we were living in a nation almost completely organized around the automobile.

Now the same thing is going on. We're all *reorganizing* around the digital revolution. And, in many ways, it's faster and a lot less gradual.

For example, think of how many of your current behaviors are now software-based. That's huge.

So the first thing we'll tell you to do on what will be a growing life-long-list of Things To Do, is to make a start at learning all you can about today's fast-changing marketplace.

You really have to do it. Sure, we can tell you things that were somewhat true and useful a few years ago, but information like that is almost more dangerous than no information at all.

It's changing. Fast. Stay alert.

Learn all you can. OK, time for Change #2.

Revolutionary Change #2: The New Normal.

There's one thing we do know. This reorganization is all part of the larger shift to digital.

Just as our whole society reorganized around the automobile, we are deep in the process of reorganizing ourselves around digital technology: Wi-Fi. Mobile. High Definition. GPS.

You're kind of used to it – but it's really all quite new, and we're still in the process. Those two changes – the marketplace and digital – are rubbing up against each other in all kinds of new ways – with all kinds of new consequences.

It's making revolutionary changes in our behavior – and it's changing career choices. For example… you now have a relationship – with a mobile digital device.

Bet you've checked it within the last thirty minutes.

In terms of the history of civilization, that's a brand new behavior. And it's everywhere.

Your media and information consumption is still evolving – with a number of behavioral varieties.

For example… are you an earbud person – one of those who walks down the street seeming to talk to yourself (we know, you're on the phone).

Or do you text? Is video calling a part of your life? A big part or a small part? Email, real mail, shop online, greet online, meet online, or…

These days, we're swimming in data, and using software to stay afloat. All of this is a big change in your life – and a part of how the whole world is changing.

While you're at it, you might want to look at a short speech on the topic – by me – on video. http://www.adbuzz.com/video/T42Day1.mov

It's on our adbuzz.com website – enough said.

Thought For The Day

Things To Do:

- Make a quick list of your digital behaviors.

- Which are the newest ones?

- What software are you using?

- What software should you get – and learn?

- Go to www.adbuzz.com Take a look at that video – it's Thought for the Day #1. It's in CAFÉ.

OK, how about some

Discussion Topics:

(Class discussion, or… short essays if your teacher wants to have something to grade.)

- **Change #1: The 21st Century Marketplace.** How do you see the marketplace changing and reorganizing?
  What are the most important aspects of the marketplace in your life right now?
  How might these changes impact your future career choice? Short term? Long term?

- **Change #2: The New Normal.** How is digital technology changing your behavior?
  What are currently the most important pieces of digital technology in your life?

- What might the next one be?

2. Build Your Brand.
Build Your Brain.

HUH? Yes, that's one of the things this book is about.

We're not only going to help you build a marketing personality, a "brand," but we're going to help you build up some of your mental skills – ones that are just kicking in.

Two things are happening inside your head – where that thinking tool between your ears is located.

First, you're developing a higher order of decision-making skills. Maybe you've heard of "teen brain," and maybe you haven't. Google it if you want. That's OK, we'll wait.

The basic fact is that new levels of decision-making skills are kicking in. Obviously, it's a bit different from person to person, but the key is that you're developing new mental abilities. This will continue.

Second, you're starting to accumulate more information – and a lot of it is interesting to you – a lot more interesting than it might have been a few years ago.

That will also continue.

Your college and university years are times when you are starting to accumulate a lot of this new information, and, better yet, beginning to figure out what to do with it.

That's what's going on inside your brain as you work your way through this book, and then onto the road ahead.

You'll be developing skills – skills that will be useful in the years ahead – and accumulating and organizing information that is going to be useful as well.

Though, at this stage, it's not always clear exactly which information is really useful and what is just taking up space on your brain's bookshelf. Hard to tell, isn't it?

So... this book is going to focus on a few ways to change your brain. Seriously. They are the following:

- **A change in the relationship between your hand and your brain.** We're going to bring back handwriting. And, for some of you, we're going to improve your printing. Yes, we know that we're moving to digital and video, but you will find that improving your basic hand skills, as well as your visual/design sense, will make everything work better.

- **A change in how you think about communication.** Right now, you're focused – correctly – on what to say. Well and good. But we're going to expand that. When we're done, you'll start paying more attention to how the messages that you send are *received.*

- **A change in how you look at the world.** When you go through a small town, do you wonder how it functions? Where do people work? What do they do?

If you see a lot of empty store fronts, do you wonder what's going on? Your career will have you connecting in a positive way with the marketplace around you. Pay attention!

Where are those new opportunities showing up?

What are the things we should avoid?

Can we fill that empty storefront with a hot new startup, or should we go look for opportunity somewhere else?

When you see a TV commercial, do you think about the business model behind that message? Most people don't.

Think of that TV screen as a ventriloquist act. Most people just pay attention to the dummy – not the business behind the scenes – pulling strings and paying bills.

You need to expand your view and start seeing "the game behind the game." And a few other changes...

- **A change in the way you view yourself.** As the saying goes, *"it's hard to read the label when you're inside the bottle."* That's true for all of us.

Let's try to improve our vision and our perspective. Part of being successful in this increasingly complicated world means we need to develop a better exterior view of who we are.

In addition, to some degree, we need to make ourselves just a bit more distinctive and memorable. Essentially, that's what this "Brand You!" thing is all about.

Let's not go overboard on this, but let's be clear – the purpose of this book is to help you become a more successful "product" in the career marketplace of human beings in the 21st Century.

Things To Do:

OK, this will be another one of those "quick think" sections. But it covers some fairly important concepts. So give these a bit of time.

Then again, don't worry that you'll forget. We're going to be hammering on these concepts for the rest of this book.

- **A change in how your hand and brain relate.**

- **A change in how you think about communication.**

- **A change in how you look at the world around you.**

- **A change in how you view yourself.**

Discussion Topic.

- **"Teen Brain."** We began with a mention of "teen brain." What is that? In general, how do you think your mental processes and capabilities are changing?

3. Career Gear Stage 1:

SO, WHAT'S YOUR "OP?" Your what?

Your OP – your *Online Presence.* It's the sum total of what you're doing and who you are in that expanding inter-linked world of digital information.

OK, this is a fairly long chapter and this time you're going to have to do some stuff – not just sit there and think about it.

Here's a Quick Checklist: Long term, this is where you and your "OP" need to be headed. Ready?

- **Personal graphics:** Personal Brand Icon, Business Card, "3-Up," Shipping labels (if necessary). Promotional items?

- **Brand Strategy/Brand Story:** We'll get to these, but they will be a key part of your "Go To Market" program.

- **Online.** Personal URL for website (you may not be using it yet, but you ought to reserve something now). Your site will contain your online portfolio.

  Also… your Facebook page. Your LinkedIn profile. And additional "social media" (Twitter, blog, podcast, etc.). This is going to be a moving target – you'll need whatever social media platform fits with you and your "brand."

- **Deliverables:** These will be items related to who you are – not just as a brand, but as someone who can make a real and positive contribution in your chosen field. They may exist online, but, in the main, they should also be tangibiles.

  For example, if you're involved with a band, there may be a website and downloadable tunes. The tangibles would be: a poster, a CD, and promotional items, like a T-shirt or the band's logo on a hat. If you're involved with a charity or nonprofit. Ditto.

We'll cover some of this in a bit more detail in *Chapter 27, Twelve Kinds of Portfolios.*

But for now, here are a few tools I want you to have.

By the way, this is not optional.

Tool Group #1: Writing Instruments You Like.

We don't want cheap ballpoints or pencils that won't sharpen. My personal choice – the Pentel Felt Tip Sign Pen– I buy 'em by the box.

These might not be the best for you – they dry out too quick. But you do want something that makes a stronger mark than the typical bank ballpoint.

You might try a medium-weight ballpoint – black – with a gel ink. Or a fountain pen – one where the metal nub actually changes to match your own personal writing stroke.

Actually, you're going to want to work in three weights:

- **Fine.** Use this for note writing, longer work, and editing. In my view, black is better than blue. You might also want to get a red one for edits and revisions.

- **Medium.** You're in a meeting. Or you need to write something on a Post-It. You're going to need something stronger than a ballpoint. It should project a strong simple line – to go with your soon-to-be-improved handwriting.

  Let's say you need to write the name and address of an important person on an envelope – and getting it done on a printer will be a problem. How is that envelope – addressed by you – going to look?

- **Heavy.** You'll need to write at this weight when you address packages or big envelopes. You'll need it when you post ideas that need be read across the room.

You know, that BIG IDEA you're going to have in the meeting that will be key to pulling the campaign together.

Usually, a black Sharpie will get it done. You'll need some kind of marker. Be sure to keep the top on tight.

They dry out quick if you forget.

Tool Group #2: 3x5 Cards, Pads, Post-its, Notebooks, and, of course, Paper.

- **3x5 Cards.** For a start, buy a pack of 3x5 cards. You might also want to buy one of those "pocket portfolios" to hold the ones you're carrying around. Use 'em for jotting down ideas, presentations on the spot, To Do lists, project notes, and so on. Lined, plain, color – find out what's right for you.

- **Pads.** Unless you're an art director, you won't need those expensive layout and tracing pads. And, let's face it, not everything we think is 8.5" x 11." See what works for you – there are a lot more pad designs and sizes out there. As you develop your "brand" and your "voice" you'll start to find something you prefer. Lined. Unlined. Graph Paper.

- **Post-Its.** Gotta have 'em. You might want to gravitate to a color (yellow is probably the default). You'll use small ones to identify important ideas in books and background materials. You'll want to stick one on the door to your room if you suddenly had to go grab a latte.

  And… if someone you work with did a nice job, put it on a Post-it and let 'em know. A nice note never hurt.

Tool Group #3: Presentation Programs & Materials.

- **PowerPoint (or Keynote).** You need to become fairly competent at some presentation program. I kind of cut my teeth on PowerPoint – I like Keynote better for the looks – and if you find something that does a better job for you – fine. Just be sure you can use it wherever you need it.

- **Materials.** Know what a "dongle" is? That's that silly little plug-connector thing that hooks your computer up to the projector, or the A/V system, or whatever. Well, those silly things are serious business.

    There are a lot of different ones – and they seem to change with every generation – you need to be sure you have the ones you need.

Or, you'll be like me – giving a speech in South Bend, IN – without the right dongle. Or that Las Vegas presentation where the audio only worked with one laptop and the video only worked with the other. Yikes! Good thing I had that back-up.

I gave the speech hitting both buttons at the same time.

You probably need to have a little bag that holds dongles, spare plugs, maybe a spare flash drive, USBs for the various bits of gear you use.

And maybe a bandage or two.

Tool Group #4: *To Do.

That's the name of the text file you're going to start – *To Do – the asterisk (*) will keep it at the front of your file list. You should open it every day.

Many of you may already be using a productivity app, like Evernote or Wunderlist or any of the other dozens of apps that are out there. Well and good.

You should also use one of the calendar apps that will help remind you of the appointment two weeks from now that is too easy to forget.

However… in addition to whatever app you might use - whether it's bare bones or full of bells and whistles, you should have a simple text file that gives you an historical record.

Why? First, because it's not an app - limited by screen size of some setting - like the multiple To Do lists that some have.

Second, it's yours. You don't have to make your list fit the app, you make the text file fit you.

Third, you now have back-up. Apps can go down, cell phones can go missing. and each app has its strengths and weaknesses – some are good for complex projects, others work best for grocery lists. A bit of what some call "redundancy," can make your To Do function more "robust." So…

List the things that you want to do in a way that makes sense (alphabetical – by category, whatever). You'll probably have categories - good. List the things you want to get done: for your course work, for your social life, for your career.

That's not all you'll want to list. How about books you want to get around to reading. Things you want to send to people you like. Things you want to do. Thank you notes to others.

And maybe notes to yourself.

Try to do a little bit on this every day. Did you finish something? Good. Put a check next to it (that's Option/v on most keyboards). Then, do a cut and paste and put it at the bottom of your *To Do list.

After a while, if you've been productive, it'll get a bit long – do some sort of Save As and make a fresh one – I usually do two a year.

You may already have something else that works for you, but as we start this Brand You! thing, why not start one more little text file?

An asterisk* will put it on the top of the list – and "To Do" is a nice reminder that you ought to be doing something.

Things To Do: Career Gear 1:

Time to do some shopping. Here's what you'll need:

Tool Group #1: Writing Tools. Three kinds.

Over time, your preferences may change, but let's get started. And, unless you've already given this lots of time and attention, you probably need to revise your current writing tools.

In general, you'll want to be a bit bolder and heavier.

Your nearby university book store may have what you need (don't forget to look in the art supplies section), or you may want to go to one of those office supply superstores.

Take your time – these tools are going to be your new friends as you build your brand.

- **Your fine-line writer.** Look for a thick, comfortable barrel and a medium point. These days, black gel ink is pretty good. Once you find what you like, buy a box of 'em.

- **Medium Weight.** A good fine marker or felt tip should give you the stroke you need. Again, I like the Pentel Sign felt-tip and order them by the box. But they're a bit expensive for a student budget. Look at markers and find something you like. Try them one at a time – you'll figure it out.

  For a number of years, I used a Cross Pen with a felt tip. Not bad. Some people absolutely love fountain pens – they even collect them. You might want to see if a fountain pen works for you.

  You also might want to look for something unique for your signature. Ad legend Leo Burnett – used big thick art pencils (in the days before markers). He also used a fountain pen and signed his letters and memos with green ink.

As you can see, they still use those pencils as part of the Leo Burnett "brand."

- **Heavy Weight.** For a start, get a black Sharpie. You may find something you like better – or your medium-weight tool may do the job for you.

- **Pencils and other stuff.** I'm not a pencil person, but if they work for you, and you have a good pencil sharpener nearby, do what feels right.

Tool Group #2: 3x5 Cards, Pads, Post-its, Notebooks, Paper...

You probably have most of this already. But maybe not too many 3x5 cards. Get a packet or two. You might also want to get one of those card wallets or "pocket briefcases." They're nice.

They tuck right into a pocket, purse, or back pack. They kinda look like this… actually, they look exactly like this. There's a company called Levenger that has deluxe leather versions of these and also a nice range of cards: To Do lists, projects, Week Ahead, etc. And you can usually find a less expensive version at one of those big office supply stores. For a start, ordinary 3x5 cards will do just fine.

Tool Group #3: Presentation Stuff.

- **PowerPoint (or Keynote).** Do you have it loaded onto your computer? Good. Start getting familiar with it. BTW – if you're a designer or an art director, you won't use this program much – don't worry. And there may be new web programs that replace these standbys.

For the moment, my advice is to get reasonably good at PowerPoint – or KeyNote if you want to look a bit slicker.

- **"Dongles"** Do you have these already? If not. Get what you'll need to present with your laptop. Visual <u>and audio.</u>

Your Career Gear Checklist:

There are a lot of items on this list. But you'll be pleasantly surprised at how much you've done by semester's end.

The Basics:
- ❏ Resume´
- ❏ Business Card
- ❏ "3-Up" or stationery (We'll get to "3-Ups" very soon)

Your "OP," Online Presence:
- ❏ Personal URL
- ❏ Website
- ❏ Facebook page.
- ❏ LinkedIn profile.
- ❏ "Twesumé" (optional) 140 characters.
- ❏ Other Social Media Platforms:
  Twitter, Instagram, Pinterest, SnapChat, blog, audio podcast, _____, _____, _____, _____.
- ❏ Videos: YouTube, video podcast, Vimeo, _____, _____.

Personal Brand: (You won't have much of this… yet)
- ❏ Logo/Icon
- ❏ Photo
- ❏ Biography/Press Release
- ❏ Brand Strategy: Target, Objective, Benefit.
- ❏ Your Brand Story
- ❏ Project Samples. What are these?
- (Think of band posters, press clippings, promotional items, publicity materials, and etc.)

4. The Other Side.

TO BE AN EFFECTIVE COMMUNICATOR, you need to start seeing the world from "The Other Side." You need to develop the habit of looking at things through the eyes of the *receiver* of your message.

You also probably need to improve your understanding of those sending you messages – the ones behind the scenes – and behind the TV screen.

In conversations and relationships, you need to develop the habit of thinking about how the world looks from the other side of that conversation. And that relationship.

My Favorite Example.

What we say and how that message is received can be very different. Like the subhead says, this is my favorite example.

When someone says, *"Don't worry about the money,"* what's your immediate reaction? Of course, you instantly worry about the money. Maybe you weren't worried before, but now you are.

See what's going on? In this case, the message received is the *exact opposite* of the message sent. That's an extreme and easy-to-understand example, but the principle is one you should embrace – probably for the rest of your life.

It's not just the message, it's how it's *received.*

Hold that thought.

You need to understand the mindset and concerns of the person on the other side of the table. It should become a habit.

The Other Side of the Interview.

For example, when going in for an interview, most of us are just a bit intimidated by that stranger on the other side of the desk – the one who holds our fate in his or her hands.

Well, that's sort of true, but do you ever think about how worried the person is who is doing the interviewing? Huh?

Worried? About what?

About making a bad hire, that's what.

It happens all the time – and making the wrong hire is almost always an unhappy and expensive experience for the company.

Think about the consequences of a wrong hire. First, it takes a while to discover – after all, this seemed like the right person at the time. Second, the un-hiring and re-hiring process is very expensive in terms of time and lost efficiency.

Finally, there is what is known as "opportunity cost." The company not only lost income and efficiency when it made that bad hire, it also lost the good things that could have come from the right hire – that opportunity is lost forever.

How does this information help you?

First, you can be more friendly, caring and sympathetic toward the person on the other side of the table.

Second, you now understand the real challenge – to help that person understand how and why you just might be the right hire. (If you're not, let's move along.)

How do we do that?

Understanding the Receiver.

How much do you really know about the company that you're interviewing? Hey, maybe you want to find out just a bit more about them. And maybe ask a question or two. Good idea.

What are their needs and challenges? Key clients?

For a start, just demonstrating that you've taken the time to understand the company itself and the area in which it does business – well that seems like a step in the right direction of making people think you might be the right hire.

Get the idea? Of course you do. In fact, you already do this a bit – mostly with parents and people you already know. You, as they say, "know where they're coming from."

Now you have to work to get better at quickly understanding and dealing with those you don't know very well.

If you're a designer, you'll learn to think in terms of the "user experience." Actually, we should all think that way.

Once Upon a Time...

Old story. Back when I was interviewing. Previous century. I began interviewing a year early – went to Chicago and New York agencies to "see what they were looking for."

My basic line, *"I want to know what it takes to be the kind of person you want to hire a year from now."* Who's going to say no? Well, at least it worked back then.

Not every interview was terrific, but two – in particular – taught me a lot. One guy at Ogilvy defined it all for me,. He said, *"There are three kinds of writers. One can do the body copy, one can do the next ad in the campaign, and the one we're looking for has the idea for the next campaign."* Well said.

There was a point of view at the time that the kind of thinking that created new products was the same kind of thinking that created new ad campaigns. Might still be true.

Second, I ran into the guy who ran one of the very first portfolio courses (back then, your portfolio was called your "book"). Then, I took a look at a portfolio done in one of those classes – by a young man who'd just been hired. The light went on.

I got it. I saw what you had to do.

Today, there are quite a few portfolio schools. You should take a look at what students do there – and how the portfolios look – even if that's not exactly the field you'll be entering.

You need to see what the standard is. Because, these days, just about everyone needs some sort of portfolio.

28

If you're in some sort of marketing, you'll be gathering data on the "target audience." If you're in PR, you'll learn to think more and more about "publics."

These are all variations on the same big important idea – understanding those on The Other Side.

Get good at it.

How to Be Interesting.

Finally, let's talk about the difference between being boring and being interesting. This is important.

Let's say you're at a party and you meet someone – and that person spends the next twenty minutes talking about himself – or herself. Probably himself.

Then, you meet someone else. And, miracle of miracles, that person is kind of interested in *you*. He or she is actually interested in what you think, what you do, where you're from, and what you'd like to be doing five years from now.

OK, without knowing any more than that – which one of these conversations was more interesting? Easy answer.

When you think about it, that's why the horoscope is one of the most read parts of the newspaper. Why?

Because it's about you! Again, hold that thought.

Things To Do:

- **New Habit #1.** Start thinking more about how the world looks from the other person's point of view.

- **New Habit #2.** Every time you see a commercial or read an ad, try to figure out their strategy. Sure, they all want to sell you something. But what else is going on? Try to understand "the game behind the game."

- **New Habit #3.** Get better at being interesting.

5. The Road Ahead.

FROM RÉSUMÉ TO ONLINE PRESENCE – in terms of "deliverables," the things we actually put together (and deliver) here's the path we're on.

If you take a look at our Table of Contents, you'll see that we have "The Road Ahead" listed twice. The purpose of this one is to give you a feel for what we want to do over the next few months.

As they say, *"Tell 'em What You're Going to Tell 'em. Tell 'em. Tell 'em What You Told 'em."*

This is the *"Tell 'em What You're Going to Tell 'em"* part.

At the end of this, we'll have some encouraging words about the path that you are creating for yourself.

That's the other "Road Ahead." But… first things first.

Step by Step.

Here's what we'll be doing …

- **Developing new skills and habits.** That "other side" thing we just talked about is just the beginning.

  First, you need to start paying more attention to visual stuff. Design, type, logos, and other types of visual communication. If you're going to be doing that in your career – well and good. But even if you "can't draw," you need to improve your design awareness and your ability to make graphic/visual decisions.

  Next, we're going to work a bit on your handwriting. We'll tell you a story about how your hands and your handwriting got to the state they're in. For most of you – guys in particular – we're going to take a few steps to make it better.

  This may also improve your grades and your overall mental abilities – no kidding! Research says so.

Finally, you're going to take the first few steps in developing your personal brand. As time goes by, you'll probably put those first efforts in a drawer or a file – or your parents might put them on the refrigerator next to that nice little drawing from sixth grade – but you'll be getting started.

- **Start Building your "OP."** Too many leave school with a degree, a resumé, and a LinkedIn profile. That's not enough. In Career Gear I, you saw an initial checklist. We'll be working on that list.

- **Taking Your Brand to Market.** These initial tools will get us rolling – and they will be very similar for all of you. And now it's time for custom work. It's Brand You! time. Because each of you is a unique product with a fit in the marketplace. What parts are unique and what's that fit? That's what we're going to be working on.

Things To Think About:

This has been a "preview" section. In the rest of the book we'll be working on three things:

- **Skill-Building.** First, we need to improve some basics – like visual awareness, handwriting, and your first Brand You! icon.

- **Your "OP."** Next, you need to take your personal brand beyond what everybody does – make a résumé and go to LinkedIn. Things need to get more, as they say, "robust."

- **Your "Go To Market" Strategy.** We'll get you started – and wish you well as you go out on your own Road Ahead.

II. Skill-Building.

THIS IS GOING TO BE FUN. Whether you develop skills you didn't know you had – or improve some you've already got, you're going to enjoy this journey.

Best of all, they're the skills that will help you succeed in today's more visually-oriented marketplace.

Here's what's going on.

The Visual Shift.

Today, we grab more and more of our information visually.

It isn't just a "picture is a thousand words" thing, it's the fact that as the world becomes increasingly complex, visual navigation, information design, and quick-as-a-flash visual communication have become more and more necessary.

In addition, the world around us is becoming better at design. Really. Think of the intuitive simplicity of the Apple interface – it's called a GUI (Graphic User Interface). Did you know that? Pay attention. This is a big deal.

One big reason that GUI has taken over is quite simply that the processing power in computer chips has grown big enough to handle graphic processing quickly and easily.

It takes a lot more of that processing power to execute those simple "click here" commands and show you those easy-to-understand graphics. This is fairly new.

In the early days, computers were much more "CUI" – that stands for Character User Interface. There was less processing power, so you had to use character commands in a much less user-friendly environment. That was then.

As things shifted, those early graphics computers took a very long time to do what we now do quickly and simply.

"User-friendly."

Today, being user-friendly is what it's all about. Steve Jobs of Apple was one of the first to recognize that high-tech could also be friendly. It was *visual* communication, not verbal.

This also means that most of you reading this should try to make your own visual shift. Think about it.

You've been learning with words. Our educational system is centuries old and it's always been word-based.

Nothing wrong with that – but, for the most part, you've been operating in a verbal dominant mode.

What's more, you've been trained to play back what you've learned with more words. You serve up lots of words to teachers, who are paying attention to the words you use, and who are also usually operating in that same verbal mode.

Speed bump ahead. As you move toward what we'll call the "Career Stage" of your life, there will be fewer teachers paying attention, and many more people who are *not* paying attention – or who are very busy – or both. So you'd better make things very clear and much easier to understand. Right? User-friendly.

Being quick about it wouldn't hurt, either. Right?

That means you need to get better at visual communication. See?

Design is not just what it looks and feels like. Design is how it works.

Steve Jobs

33

6. Design &
"The User Experience."

YOU NEED TO "THINK DIFFERENT." As we just mentioned, you're the product of a word-based learning system that's been around for centuries.

Words come into your brain – and words come out. That's fine for a lot of things. But now we all need to get better at learning to speak a different language. We need to learn to "speak visual."

We need to understand how and where to find and use visuals to reinforce our verbal thoughts.

Why? Because when we do, we will be able to communicate more quickly, more powerfully, and more enjoyably.

Words, Graphics, Keyboards, & Hand Skills.

Knowing how to type is good – it's an important skill. It lets us get our thoughts on paper clean and quick.

In addition, a text file is pretty handy. It's easy to work with, easy to read, and easy to improve.

We can print it, send it, save it, and retrieve it later on.

But did you know that when you really want to learn something – like taking notes in a classroom – typing isn't the best way to do it? How about that?

Recent studies revealed that there seems to be something

about that good old hand/brain connection that kicks in when we write it down by hand.

We learn better, we remember better, and we think – well, sometimes better. And sometimes we just think different.

As someone who made a career of having ideas for a living, I can tell you that it is often better to have that pad and writing /drawing implement by your side as you grab that idea for the first time from wherever the heck it came from.

After you write it down – and you need to add and organize – with a bit of a strategy and initial outline – that's the time to open a fresh new text file and get it down.

But for those initial moments – you really kind of want your hand and brain working together.

Steve Jobs' Secret.

One of the reasons Apple Computer became the platform of choice for visual communication was born when Steve Jobs, one of Apple's founders, was taking classes at a university (he was auditing them). Steve took a typography course.

He came to understand how type is designed, how it works, and why it's important. From there, he went to great lengths to include strong graphic capabilities (as strong as possible given the chip capacities of the time) in every generation of Apple from Lisa on. He also "borrowed" the original GUI (which was developed by Xerox) for early Mac computers. That's Graphic User Interface.

Jobs even hired legendary designer Paul Rand (he's the guy featured in that "Think Different" poster on the previous page) to design this logo for NeXT, his short-lived computer company.

Jobs worked to make the operating system

a graphic powerhouse. It was. And NeXT lives on.

Because when Steve re-joined Apple, that NeXT operating system (NeXTSTEP) became the heart of Apple's OSX operating system. Design counts.

In fact, it seems to count now more than ever. Think of successful brands like Apple, Starbucks, and Target. When you do, design components come to mind. Right?

Top "B" schools (Business schools) like Stanford are now adding "D" (Design) components to the curriculum.

See where we're going with this? As you work to establish your own personal brand, you'll probably need to have some effective design elements.

Some you'll create, some you'll borrow, and, in the beginning, some you'll copy – as you learn. The legendary art director Helmut Krone (the famous Volkswagen ad campaign was one of his), recommended this...

"I'd like to propose a new idea for our age: Until you've got a better answer, you copy. I copied Bob Gage for five years. I even copied the leading between his lines of type. And Bob originally copied Paul Rand, and Rand first copied a German typographer named Tschichold.

"The thing to do... is to find an honest answer. Solve the problem. Then, if through the years a personal style begins to emerge, you must be the last to know. You have to be innocent of it." Thanks for the good advice, Helmut.

Start to study the design around you. See what you like and use that as your starting point. The more you do this, the more your taste will develop, and the better you'll get.

Most likely, none of us will become design legends like Paul Rand or Helmut Krone. But we can develop an appreciation for what good is – and we can make use of it.

That's what Steve Jobs did.

OK, this next subhead is important.

"The User Experience."

That's how a good designer looks at the problem – or assignment. A designer looks at it through the eyes of the *user.*

Designers have been operating from "the other side" for years. Sometimes, the result is one you barely notice.

For example, at its best, our highway signage is so clear  that it's functionally invisible – or transparent. We can get to virtually any major city or town on our highway system – just by following those signs.

White sans serif on green. Easy-to-read. Easy-to-understand.

Sure, it's nice to have GPS, but good design can help you navigate the entire United States of America.

As our world gets more complicated, clear and well-designed navigation is becoming more and more important whether it's your website, the menu at the place you just had lunch, or looking for the exit for that job interview.

More and more, good design counts.

Hold that thought.

Things To Do:

- **New Habits. Reading Material.** Take a look at some design magazines: *CA (Communication Arts)* and *HOW* are good places to start. *CA* has a "Design Annual," wall-to-wall "eye candy." Also, *WIRED* and *Business Week* have annual design issues – they're worth owning. and, you can usually access some of the back issues online.

You should also take a look at the Awards Books section at an art supply store – you might be pleasantly surprised at what you find. Look and learn.

- **New Habits. A Clip File**. Back in the old days, you just had flimsy file folders and tore pages out of magazines. Now you can add a folder on your computer. Call it "Good Examples" – or something like that – save screen grabs or jpgs, or PDFs, or links.

- **New Habits. Take an Intro Design Course or Buy a Book.** There are a lot of them online now. Some of them are free. And there are a few books that are pretty good.

  The big thing that's going to happen is that, as you start to pay attention to design – whatever level you're currently working at – you will absolutely get better.

  You'll develop better judgment and who knows, you might even get good at it. But until you do – try to copy the good stuff – just like Helmut told us.

Discussion Topic.

- **Bring in Some Design Examples.** A napkin. A menu. A poster. A T-shirt. A CD cover. A magazine. An ad. There's design all around us.

  Let's spend a bit of time talking about the job design is doing. Why do you like it? What does it do for you?

  Do you notice design decisions?

7. Making Your Mark.

IT'S CALLED BRANDING. So… how are you branding your communications? Seriously.

Is there anything distinctive? Is it attractive? Does it look cool? Contemporary? Is it an authentic reflection of who you are and "what you bring to the party?" Probably not yet.

See where we're going on this?

Three Tasks.

In this next sequence, we're going to work on three things.

- **Developing your Brand Icon.** This will be your first and it probably won't be the last.

- **Improving Hand Skills.** We're going to help you work on your handwriting – and tell you a story about how the school system let you down years ago.

- **The "3-Up."** You're going to create, design, and produce your first personal brand tool – an easy-to-make, easy-to-use piece of personal communication.

Now let's talk a bit more about "Making Your Mark."

Mediums and Messages.

Marshall McLuhan, the media guru, tells us to think of things as *extensions*. The car extends our feet, clothes extend our skin, the telephone extends our voice. Got it?

Now, let's apply that concept to media and the messages we receive and send.

Media extends our senses. Books extend our brains, video helps us see farther, radio extends our ears…

On the same token, the media tools we use, phones, email, selfies, and Facebook profiles, extend us.

So we're going to be working on paying a bit more attention to how we extend ourselves in the digital media universe.

We'll get to it in a minute.

This is the end of this very short chapter.

Time for a quick think.

Discussion Topic.

- **"Extensions."** This may be a new way of thinking about things – but it's kind of cool. Let's think about it.
  What are the main ways you "extend" yourself in today's digital media environment?

- **"Obsolescence."** This will also make you think.
  OK, we understand how the digital camera on our phones made the traditional camera kind of obsolete – and that's why Kodak, which was a huge company, went bankrupt, and is now much smaller.

"The Flip."

So here's a McLuhan-esque way of understanding the flip side of extensions. Cars extend our legs – but when we get in a car it's like they were amputated and we're in a giant wheelchair.

No worries. We get out of the car and our legs are back.

But, as the Internet extends us, do we turn our backs and amputate relationships that are right next to us?

Hey, it happens. Best friends from grade school may not last through high school. Best friends in high school – well, sometimes it's hard to keep connected.

But – as you extend yourself – don't cut things off simply because you didn't think about it.

8. Your Brand Icon.

LET'S GET STARTED DEVELOPING your personal brand.

Perhaps you've already got something. Your initials. Some little drawing or thing that's sort of you – maybe it's already on your Facebook profile. Well, even if you already have something, let's see what else we can come up with.

Remember, we're now in more of a digital visual environment, and not so long from now, when our résumé hits someone's desk, when our portfolio shows up on someone's screen, or when we need to be distinctive in a world full of résume´s and LinkedIn profiles – how are we measuring up?

Color – Animal – Place.

Here's a fun way for you to start – it's also sort of party game… Think of a color, an animal, and a place.

Got it? (By the way, I'm Green - Gorilla - Portland, OR)

You now have some raw material for your brand.

By the way, this is not science, but it's interesting.

- The color is sort of how you view yourself.

- The animal is sort of how you think people view you.

- The place represents your ideal mind state. (I really like hanging out in Portland on a misty afternoon, with a hot cup of coffee and a book at Powell's.)

You've got three initial pieces for your icon. What else?

More Stuff for the Stew.

We're making this recipe up as we go along.

You've got initials. Hobbies. Things you like to do. Favorite music and favorite bands.

The school you go to – favorite sports teams. And – even

though you are a work in progress – just kind of who you are.

Are you starting to collect thoughts?

What else do you like to do? I played saxophone in high school and college. Wasn't great – but I wasn't awful, either. Had a nickname – Zoot. It was fun.

I developed a few rough graphics around that.

When I had my first creative consulting practice – many years later – my business card was a light bulb with a cartoon drawing of my face on it.

Your turn.

How Do I Do This?

You may still be asking yourself this question.

And, of course, the answer is you do it by doing it.

There are no right or wrong answers, but there is better and worse, and you're going to be changing over the years.

At the end of this section – The 3-Ups, I'll show you some of the answers I've come up with.

But, for now, grab that writing thing – and maybe a few 3x5 cards. Start making a list. Got some things in mind? You can do it.

My cousin (by marriage) is a jazz musician of some note – Richie Cole – here's his brand icon. He's a be-bop alto player.

The brand for his band is Alto Madness."

A little rough? That's OK, it's real and it's Richie. He has it on his Alto Madness Orchestra music stands.

If you knew Richie, you'd know this was a pretty good fit. Incidentally, his best album was probably *Hollywood Madness* – done with The Manhattan Transfer.

42

Things To Do:

OK, enough thinking. Time for some doing.

- **Collect thoughts and images for your Brand Icon.**
Got a computer file? Good. Pull everything together into a
folder. Look at it. Add new thoughts and images. Now print
'em out.

- **Scan some stuff.** Do some roughs. Create some rough
representations of your brand icon. As thought-starters, you
can grab scans and stuff from the Internet – but, please no
trademarked or copyrighted stuff. No Mickey Mouse. No
Marvin the Martian. That's OK for Facebook – not for this.

- **Monogram.** Create a logo based on your name or initials.
A monogram isn't the worst place to start.

- **Color. Animal. Place.** Take another look at that. Maybe
something will hit you. (I've got a drawing somewhere of
me like a gorilla – not quite – but interesting.)

- **Take a Look. Let it Cook.** OK, you've got some stuff –
now stick it in the back of that fine brain – or show it to
some friends. Know anyone who's a designer? Buy 'em a
cup of coffee. Heck, buy 'em dinner.

9. Hand Skills.

HOW'S YOUR HANDWRITING? If it's already first-rate, my apologies for this next chapter. But my guess is it's mediocre at best. That's the case for most of us – particularly the guys.

Now I'll tell you a story about why that's true.

The Wrong Skill at the Wrong Time.

Think back. Remember when you sat in first grade and learned to print? And then later you did those loopy things and learned to write what we call "cursive."

If you were a boy, I'm pretty sure you probably just cursed. Here's why. Your muscles weren't ready!

At that age – six or seven – we're all still growing. For boys, your larger muscle groups are coming along – you run, climb trees, throw a ball, play sports. But not the fine motor skills.

If you're a girl, your small muscle groups are coming along – you can do finer work with your fingers – beads, dolls, tea parties... that kind of stuff.

Well guess what? When they first put that writing thing in your hands, most boys are simply not very good at it. You try – but it just looks awful. Your small muscles aren't really ready.

Meanwhile, a lot of the girls are doing pretty loop-de-loops and it all looks better – their muscle groups are ready for it and they get the gold stars.

Certainly there is some variation – a few boys will have fine motor skills that kicked in earlier, and a few girls who are, as we say, "late bloomers," won't be doing very good loop-de-loops. But, for the most part, that's what happens in the American school system.

Then, at most schools, that's it. You spend the rest of grade school and high school with whatever you were stuck with.

And, for the most part, nobody tries to make it better.

I was talking to a niece who teaches in one of the better high schools, she nodded her head sadly and agreed.

They really don't teach that stuff any more.

Then, as soon as you can use a keyboard, you go there – so you won't embarrass yourself any more.

So… are you proud of your handwriting? Thought so.

It's time to change that.

At this point, all of you have fairly well-developed fine motor skills – and pretty good learning skills – so I'm hoping you're motivated.

Now, when you decide to pay attention to this task, you are going to get pretty good at it pretty quickly. Let's go!

Branding Your Hand.

When something you wrote by hand hits somebody's desk – or somebody's mailbox – or it sits on the wall as a suggestion – or it's on a note or a card that says thanks or congratulations – how does it look?

Unless you already make a living addressing wedding invitations, I'm guessing it doesn't look terrific – particularly for the guys. Actually, my sister did address invitations – she took a calligraphy course and has a lot of fun with it.

I'm also guessing everybody sees where we're going with this. But before I give you some exercises – and teach you a whole new way to print – let's agree on some simple and fairly easy to achieve objectives.

Three Kinds of Handwriting.

There are a number of ways you'll need handwritng skills in the years to come. Three tasks for sure: Taking notes. Making a point. Signing your name.

OK, one at a time.

1. Fast and smart.
You'll need this for taking notes. Use lined paper.

You're in class. You're in a meeting. You're studying. You're at a coffee house… just thinking.

You need to be able to put it down clearly, in a fairly fast and efficient way. And you need to be able to read what you wrote when you get back to it.

Significant studies tell us that doing it by hand helps you learn better than typing it in.

Not only that, but even if you don't look at the notes afterward, those same studies tell us that writing it down by hand seems to do a better job of sticking it in your brain – so you remember better. How about that?

2. Strong and clear.
Think Post-it. Let's say you need to write a note.

Maybe it's an important call – or maybe you'll be back in half an hour – whatever.

We want you to have a strong, attractive, easy-to-read, and impossible-to-misunderstand hand. To help you do that, we're going to teach you a whole new way to print.

We think you'll like it.

3. Uniquely You.
Sign here. Nobody's asking you for your autograph yet, but whether it's signing the letter – which you typed and revised – or putting it on the greeting card you remembered to send – or – best of all – putting down a real nice version of your signature, scanning it, and then inserting it at the end of those letters – your brand needs a good signature.

It might even be your whole brand – like this guy.

Two well-known advertising executives – David Ogilvy and Leo Burnett – used their signatures as part of their agencies' branding. Ogilvy used it as the logo.

And I remember a classy ad guy I worked with in Washington DC – Harant Soghigian (Harry) had a kind of unique signature, and Sam (Sarah Ann Macuga), the Exec AD turned it into a very nice logo for the letterhead and business cards.

A color can be nice. Ogilvy used red. Leo used green ink for his signature. Harry's was kind of a hip blue-green.

Let's Give Your Handwriting a Hand.

We'll get to my printing tricks in a minute – I don't want to screw up the habits of a lifetime, but here are some ways you can improve your handwriting – whatever it is.

1. **Try different writing tools.** You need to teach your hand (and body) some brand new habits – so we need to help by changing a few things. We're all able to write a bit better – or worse – with different writing tools. You just bought some new ones – now we're going to try them out. In general, I'd go for something with a thicker barrel than what you've been using, and an easy-flow ink – like one of those new gel pens.

2. **Get a Grip.** Adjust the shape of your hand. In general, your pen or pencil should be held between your thumb and index and (optional) middle fingers. Lefties, you just have to deal with it. Don't hold it too tightly or loosely – that's why I recommend giving yourself a thicker barrel – you won't cramp up.

3. **Fingers, wrist, elbow, shoulder.** Most people don't use enough of their body to write. Pay attention to this part. Find a solid but comfortable chair at a table that's the right

height for your own height and start to analyze what you're doing. You may have some habits from years ago.

For a start, don't write with your fingers – you'll cramp up and your letters will look cramped. You should be comfortable up through to your elbow. You won't be making big moves with your elbow – but the whole structure should be in a groove – comfortable.

In fact, some of what you do is going to go all the way up to the shoulder – not big moves, small ones, your whole body should start to feel a comfortable part of the process.

If you don't feel quite right – or you're feeling kind of pressured and cramped – stretch and see what's going on. You need to find your own comfort zone. Good posture and the occasional stretch – always. By the way, good posture is often easier said than done.

If we're at the keyboard a lot, we can get that cramped up thing in our shoulders.

These days, I wear an AlignMed shirt, which pulls back against that too-tight-from-too-much-writing-or-typing feeling. (They have 'em for both guys and gals.)

Fingers. You'll have better control and a better writing angle if your pen rests over or just forward of the bottom knuckle on your index finger, not between thumb and index finger.

Wrist. This should be a relaxed supportive part of the process – let it channel your actions all the way through the...

Elbow & Shoulder. Now it gets interesting. Think about it. You want to be slightly involved all the way up to what they call the "shoulder girdle." There are small muscles all the way up in your shoulder that help you get it done.

An Exercise – some people say to try writing big letters in the air – never did it myself – but whatever it takes to unlearn old habits that aren't helping and learn new ones is probably a good idea.

1. **Line-Up.** Use lined paper – pay attention to letter size and keep your writing going horizontally. Some people go so far as to use a light box with lined paper underneath to get that nice effect. Writing that doesn't stay straight makes it look like you can't.

2. **Look to other handwriting styles for inspiration.** Now you're starting to pay attention. Anybody you know who has really nice handwriting? See what they're doing. Go onto font websites and look for handwriting samples you like. Copy each style of handwriting that you can. As you start to study other styles, you can pick and choose certain aspects of different handwritings you happen to like.

3. **Slow down and practice.** Write alphabets. Either as cursive – or as separate letters. We're also going to develop a printed style – which some of you might like better.

4. **Practice some more.** Write paragraphs and inspirational stuff. Original ones if you'd like. Something from famous speeches. Song lyrics. Perhaps a poem or an inspirational something. (My wife likes, *"To those leaning on the sustaining infinite, today is big with blessings."* And *Invictus.*) The idea is don't get hung up thinking about the content of what you write – so you can focus on the writing itself.

Do this and you <u>will</u> develop better handwriting.

Now I'm going to show you a whole new way to print. You'll thank me later. But not right away.

Give 'em the Hook! A New Way to Print.

It's called lines and hooks. I have no idea where I learned it, but for me – someone with fairly awful handwriting – it was like a new world opening up. Hey, I can read what I wrote!

Some of you may switch to this style full time – others will just use it for printing those Post-it Notes and package labels.

Here's how it works – *Every letter can be made with a simple combination of hooks and lines.*

Nothing fancy. No loop de loops running together. Just a simple hook, and a line – short or long. That's it.

You use it for the lower-case letters. Each one is just a quick simple hook/line combo. Here goes…

a – hook/short line   b – line/hook

c – hook   d – hook/line

e – hook/small line (see what's going on here?)

f – line w. hook at top + short line

g – hook/descending line ending in hook

h – line/hook   i – line + a dot

j – descending line ending in hook + a dot

k – line + two short lines   l – line

m m – line + two small "hump" hooks

n n – line + one small "hump" hook

o o – two hooks – pay attention to this one
— it's a whole new way to make a nice round "o."

p p – line/hook

q q – hook/line

r – short line/little hook

s – hook/hook – or – with this one you can do the same old squiggle you've been doing for years – but you'll see it fitting in with the other letters you're writing.

t t – line/small line
(put a hook at the bottom of the "t" if you want.)

u u – hook line

v v – line/line

w w – line/line/line/line
— kind of a quick zig-zag

x x – line/line

y y – long line/short line

z z - line/line/line

Do each one a few times – it's easy.
Then, do alphabets. A lot of them.

1234567890

Numbers – in general, just keep doing what you've been doing – though you may find yourself making that 6 and 9 more like a line/hook thing. With one exception…

The Four-Hook 8! I learned this from my Executive Art Director, Roy Sandstrom (you'll notice this book is dedicated to Roy) His 8's always looked great – and he showed me. Four hooks – not an awkward infinity sign. Do four hooks like this - and they come out really nice. See!

Now... Practice!

Write alphabets. Do it whenever you have a minute.

Soon, you'll start to feel good about your printing. Really.

Do it at a size that's right for you – most lined paper will work – though some of us use every other line.

Things To Do:

- **Work on those new writing habits.** Get comfortable and try to commit to a new more comfortable writing mode. See how your handwriting is improving? (We hope so.)

- **Practice. Practice. Practice.** Use those new writing tools, and see how you like your new printing style.

UPPER CASE IS EASY.
ABCDEFGHIJKLMN
OPQRSTUVWXYZ

10. The 3-Up.

THIS IS YOUR FIRST *BRAND YOU!* PROJECT. It's an easy-to-design, easy-to-produce and easy-to-use replacement for personal stationery.

It's a note card 3.33 inches wide and 8.5 inches high – about the size of a #10 envelope. Fits nice.

It can get produced easily at almost any copy shop, with three in a row printed out on card stock and then cut in thirds. That's why I call it a "3-Up."

Here's one of my recent 3-Up production jobs.

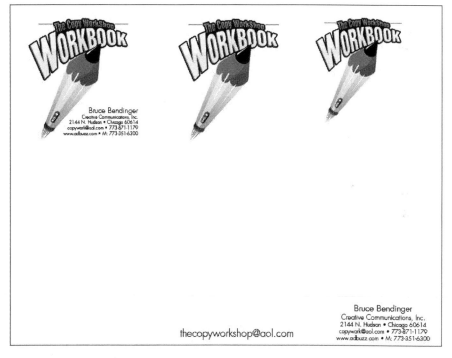

The design? That's pretty easy, too. You take your initial brand icon and put it at the top of the page – three times – and, as you can see, you can try a few variations. See what works.

Then – depending on what you want to put where – you put in whatever contact information you think is appropriate or necessary. Your email and mobile phone probably. Your address. Or – just your email. Up to you. Hey, it's yours.

Some of your contact information may change from school year to school year, so don't print a ton of 'em – 30 cards gives you 90 3-Ups. That should be plenty – for a while.

Step One. Your Brand Icon.

By now, I've got a bunch of 3-Ups. I have the "rocket pencil" – which relates to my book and publishing company.

Lower right is the one I use for personal communication.

It's my "BeBop Martini" graphic. The olive in the martini glass is also a musical note – with a red pimento. To add to the gag, it says NOTE CARD. Get it? Musical note. Note card. Not subtle.

I've got kind of a "Mad Man + music" reputation, so it works fine.

But if I'd used this graphic years ago, it might have said "young drunk." So be careful.

And here's the brand icon for my wife, Lorelei.

It was done by our good friend Cathy Grisham. (Thanks, Cathy.) It started out as stationery and a business card – but it's often too much of a big deal to use stationery. Do you fill the whole page – with what?

Then you have to type it up.

Plus, you need all of that address/Dear Sir/Sincerely stuff.

With a 3-Up, you can just throw in a note with an article you liked. And there's just enough room to say "Thought you'd find this article interesting." Or, "thanks." Or, "check enclosed." Whatever.

3-Ups are more functional than stationery – easy-to-do and easy-to-change if you have a better idea.

Sometimes, the graphic will work better on the bottom. Here's one we did for a nonprofit – The Czech Legion Project. Is that a cool train, or what? Sort of Darth Vader on rails.

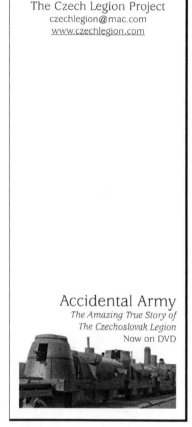

The Czech Legion Project
czechlegion@mac.com
www.czechlegion.com

Accidental Army
The Amazing True Story of
The Czechoslovak Legion
Now on DVD

Step Two. Production.

It's easy, but there are a few variations.

These days, I'll use InDesign, with a small bit of fiddling in Photoshop. But you can do it in Word – just set your document at 3 columns. Insert and center the graphic. Add informational copy. Do the same thing in each column.

Or, if you have some variation – do that.

Then, save it as a PDF. That's a standard setting. Put the PDF file on a Flash Drive. You're good to go.

The first time around, you might have to explain what you want to the person at the copy shop. These days, they know me and it's kind of "you again?"

Color costs a bit more than black and white – but even if it's just a spot of color (like the musical note in the martini), it looks better. Go for it.

First time out, don't get too many – because you're going to see ways to improve it right away.

Now look for excuses to send 'em.

Think of it as "building your brand."

What About Envelopes?

Good question. Envelopes are a pain.

If you've ever ordered them for stationery, you know that you get a lifetime supply – and they cost a lot. Those little address stickers with your name aren't bad – and – if you're willing to go through the nonsense, printing up some of those Avery custom labels could work.

Some printers do a nice job on envelopes. You can build the graphic and print 'em as you need them. Often, they can do addresses as well – and if your printer does that, see if you can't get an organized procedure in place.

The point is, you shouldn't let envelope logistics or postage (still a bargain), keep you from staying connected – or better yet – growing your network.

We'll be talking about this more a bit later in this book – but the point is worth making – repeatedly.

Positive connections with others – call it networking, call it whatever you want – is part of how we make our way in the world. Putting a 3-Up in an envelope with some other bit of accompanying something-or-other is a nice way to get started. That reminds me, I need some more envelopes.

And when it's time for stationery...

Eventually, you'll need to write a few letters – mostly cover letters when you're on the job hunt. The graphics on the 3-Up will get you started.

That nice brand icon you're developing – now you can take that graphic file and imbed it in a text document.

You now have stationery! No muss. No fuss.

Things To Do:

Hey, your first Brand You! tool! Let's do it!

* Establish your first Brand Icon.

* Put it on a 3-Up in a size and position you like. Or try a few variations. It looks a bit different when they're trimmed.

* Add appropriate contact info.

* Do a proof first, then produce 30 of 'em. (That's 10 x 3.)

* Send a few out. And, if you like what you've done, send one to me. Or, have your instructor collect 'em from the whole class and send me a packet. A note would be nice.

11. Getting Better.

TIME FOR A GENERIC PEP TALK. We all have to start somewhere. And, if you're any good, you'll do better this year than you did last year. Keep it up.

So… congratulations on your first personal brand tactic – the 3-UP –and let's take a moment to enjoy it.

Use it. Smile about it. Send a copy to your parents with a nice note. And then…

Figure out if you could make it better.

How's the type? Did you make a good decision? Is it a little too tricky? Do you still look like an amateur?

How's your brand icon? Is it slick and polished? Or, as my wife would comment when young women brought in their not-quite-ready-for-prime-time fashion designs … *"loving hands at home."* That means unprofessional.

Getting Feedback. And Using It.

One of the things we all have to learn is to how take criticism in a positive way – and then make the darn thing better.

And, even though not all criticism is accurate, warranted, or useful – a lot of it is. If you can learn to learn from it, you will keep getting better. And that's today's topic.

If you can't learn from it, or you just don't want to hear criticism, you'll be in one of those *"repeating the same behavior and expecting a different result"* kind of things.

Worse yet, we don't get in the habit. In school, your work is usually "one and done." Your instructors will sometimes hand back papers and tests with comments written on them… but rarely do you actually redo anything based on the suggestions.

Well, try to get in the habit. This is something people in all kinds of careers have to do: get feedback, analyze it, and make changes based on it. At a disciplined company like P&G, that memo can go through three to five revisions.

If it's the budget memo, try over twenty revisions. Really.

This can be difficult, especially when you don't agree with some of the proposed changes. But part of many jobs involves setting your ego aside – or at least part of it.

To be successful, you have to learn to listen and use what you heard – feedback – to make it better.

Value Criticism.

Let's start with your latest work of art – your 3-Up. Can you find someone who's a designer? You might get a free type upgrade.

Can you page through some sort of graphics award book? Look back and forth between whatever it is you did and that award book. It's okay, you're not there yet.

Again. How's the proportion? How's the "polish" of your brand icon? See anything you like better? Better is good.

Get comfortable with two contradictory feelings.

1. Feeling good about what you did.

2. Not being satisfied – wondering how you might be able to do it better.

How long will you be dealing with those two contradictory feelings? Hopefully, for the rest of a long and successful career.

And One More Thing.

Your writing needs work. Award-winning writers are *always* working on improving their writing. You should do the same.

You've been writing for some time now – though much of it has been to fill the page. The book report. The essay. The term paper. The not-that-short-story.

Years of education have been pushing us to write more.

It's sort of a sign that we've been good students – and it's a way for teachers to test whether we have anything inside our youthful brains. And, youthful brains being what they are, that sort of makes sense.

But we're heading into the turn now. Out there, "they don't want no term papers." Think of what you've had to write – and maybe will for a little while yet: Research papers, scientific reports, English papers, and so on.

It should come as no surprise that academic writing is worlds away – and words away –from the kind of writing you'll be doing in the working world. So… let's get started.

How to start? Email is a good way to start. Like to write long chatty letters to a friend – or your mom – fine. But now is the time to start getting in the habit of writing in a clear, concise, professional, and personable way.

This also applies to memos, reports, and cover letters. Need a little more help – there are a number of excellent books on business writing. Here are three of them:

Writing That Works. How to Communicate Effectively in Business. By Ken Roman and Joel Raphaelson.

What Do You Mean I Can't Write? A Practical Guide to Business Writing for Agency Account Managers. By Norm MacMaster. From The Copy Workshop.

The Copy Workshop Workbook. By Bruce Bendinger

For this chapter, our "Things To Do" section is more like "Things You've Done." That's good.

Let's review.

√ Things You've Done:

How are we doing? Let's review.

√ Developed your first Brand Icon.

√ Made a commitment to improve your hand skills – particularly your printing and hand-writing.

√ Developed a piece of personal branding – a "3-Up."

Finally…

• **If your Brand Icon/3-Up is good enough – why not make it into a business card?** Think about having a few business cards made.

   But if it isn't ready yet – no rush. It's kind of okay if your 3-Up is still a bit of a "work in progress." A business card should have some polish. It should look professional.

OK, so far, so good. Next section.

III. Knowledge-Building

THIS IS AN EXCITING TIME FOR YOUR BRAIN. You're building up your knowledge base and the database in your brain. You're starting to notice new connections.

Perhaps it's something you learned in one of your courses connecting with an article you just read in a magazine, and that also connects with something your uncle said at Thanksgiving. Well, maybe not your uncle.

New concepts and information are coming in from all over the place: the media, your courses, your conversations, things you're reading, things you're seeing, and things you're thinking.

These next chapters are about getting smarter. They are:

- **StratCom & Strat Think.** Plus other important words.

- **Goal!** We need one – just like strategies need an objective.

- **You Are a Swiss Army Knife.** It's a metaphor we like.

- **Career Gear Stage 2.** Time to work on your "O.P."

- **Big Ideas: Four Thinkers Shaping The 21st Century:** Schumpeter, Moore, McLuhan, and Romer. Interesting.

- **Making Connections & Building Your Brand Database.**

- **Team Up!** Today, business is a team sport.

    Then we'll work on your Brand You! strategy. That's Part Four. Finally, we'll focus on your Brand You! portfolio. Part Five.

12. StratCom & StratThink

STRATEGIC COMMUNICATION IS COMMUNICATION WITH A PURPOSE. Whether it's advertising, MarCom, Strat-Com, or a letter home asking for money for a Spring Break trip – each is a piece of strategic communication.

Back when I was going to school – kind of the *Mad Men* era – it was a lot of advertising and a little bit of everything else.

Advertising was really the only word I needed to know. Today, there is a much wider range of opportunities – and a few more words you need to know.

The First Three Words You Need to Know.

Advertising, MarCom, StratCom. Let's start there.

It all started with *advertising* (you know what that is), but it grew into something more. A lot more.

The seed of advertising has grown into a multi-functional something we call *MarCom* – Marketing Communications.

MarCom covers a whole range of marketing activities – and most of them are hiring. More words you need to know.

MarCom: Let's See What's Inside.

Here's a quick alphabetical list of MarCom activities:

- **Advertising.** Ad agencies used to do most of this – now ads are also created by: design firms, media companies, digital providers, and internal departments that are usually (but not always) called "Creative Services."

- **Branding & Design.** The traditional design firm, which just did things like logos, letterheads, and package and store design, now works on a whole range of marketing activities. Design thinking has become much more important as a way to handle the growing range of brand "touch points."

- **Direct Marketing.** This is a discipline that combines database expertise – the list of targets – sales promotion thinking – the incentive that will get us to respond – and creative writing – the design and creation of the message that serves it up. This is growing – particularly on the internet.

- **Event/Experiential Marketing.** Think of Concerts, Festivals, and Street Fairs. Spring break is another example. Here, marketers look to get our involvement as we experience an enjoyable event. Posters, hats, T-shirts, and free samples are some of the things you see. There's a lot more that goes on behind the scenes.

- **New Media.** It might not be new to you, but that's what we call it. This refers to the whole range of digitally delivered communications. Digital? We can dig it. The growth of the Internet and all the related activities is what many of us call "New Media." As you might imagine, in this area, the job market is exploding.

- **Public Relations & Publicity.** Here, companies look to get their messages into the old-fashioned media, the kind we read and watch. Done well, PR and publicity are very cost effective, if you have a knack for that kind of writing and thinking, you can do well.

- **Sales Promotion.** Here, marketers use incentives to influence our behavior. The message is usually wrapped around the incentive (Win/Free/Save) to get us to buy.

There are other combined forms of MarCom. Such as…

- **Sports Marketing** – this is an exciting combination of all these things – Sales Promotion (think of the special events – like "Bat Day" – and the giveaways), Public Relations (all the press conferences and press releases), Direct Marketing (that's how they sell season tickets), and New Media (naturally, you want a website for the fans). See? The MarCom marketplace has opened a wide range of opportunities for those who like to communicate with a purpose.

And that's not the only kind of purposeful communication. Now we're also seeing something even broader in scope Strategic Communications. We call it *StratCom!*

StratCom = Strategic Communications

This is also communication with a purpose.

While building business through marketing is obviously an important purpose, there may be other important good reasons to communicate. For example, *Inform* and *Entertain.*

For the most part, different types of strategic communications share the same one, two, or three objectives. Sell. Inform. Entertain. Sometimes it's only one. Sometimes it's all three.

The good news? Almost everybody needs some kind of creative content to do this. Somebody has to fill those pages, computer screens, and hours of broadcast time.

When you look at the range of creative communication jobs that we need in our 21st Century economy, you can see there are a lot of interesting career opportunities.

We've briefly covered the Selling/Marketing part, now let's take a quick look at other types of "communication with a purpose." Here are some of the careers attached to those Informing and Entertaining parts of the StratCom world.

* **Information:** News – whether it's from the newspaper, a TV or radio broadcast, or your own blog. As a society, we value good information about what's happening right now. It isn't just news, education is also an important part of the

information business – we need to know about better health habits, and better ways to learn all the things there are to know. So, for example, we need a constant stream of brochures for healthcare. Annual reports. Press releases. New textbooks and other learning tools. Videos. PowerPoints. Web sites. And so on. If you have the skills to make learning and information interesting, there could be some exciting opportunities waiting for you.

- **Entertainment:** Here's yet another word to remember – *Content.* That's what some of us call the communication that fills all those media channels – movies, TV shows, articles, and more. They're songs, poems, and comedy routines. Music videos, reality shows, movies, and sitcoms.

  If you can create a clever commercial message, well there might be a few other things you can create as well. Think about it.

Put them all together and you're starting to understand all the new opportunities for everyone who is thinking about a career in communication.

Even though we're going to focus primarily on MarCom and advertising in this book, you need to realize that jobs and careers can grow in interesting new directions.

More and more, we're seeing creative careers go across the borders of the various disciplines. For example…

Years ago, a young copywriter wrote a commercial for Nike that featured basketball star Michael Jordan and the cartoon character Bugs Bunny. It was so successful that the ad writer became a screenwriter. He helped to write the movie *Space Jam.* Maybe you saw it when you were younger.

How about *Home Alone*? John Hughes, who wrote a lot of the movies you may have enjoyed, started out as an ad copywriter.

He worked just down the hall from me at Leo Burnett, and I need to tell you one thing about John at the beginning of his very successful career. He worked his tail off. John put in tough hours at the agency. Then he wrote all night. A friend of mine was the art director who worked with him for a while, and he remembers having to wake John up (he was asleep at his desk) to get some work done.

John Hughes worked hard and deserved every bit of his success. (He also deserved to live longer – take care of yourself.)

New Careers. New Combinations.

So, your first job could be the first step in a career path that takes you in all kinds of interesting directions – depending on what you're good at and what interests you.

We all have to start somewhere. But today, there are a lot more exciting opportunities related to where you might end up.

For example, you might start with a career in health care marketing, helping to introduce important new medicines, and then finding yourself writing health information designed to help mothers give their kids a better start with better nutrition – or help seniors deal with the consequences of diabetes.

You won't exactly be selling anything, but you'll be doing what is probably a more important job – because your communication will have a very good purpose. A healthy purpose.

That's StratCom – strategic communication.

OK, got it? *Advertising. MarCom. StratCom.*

That covers the growing range of opportunities that wait for you if you can deliver communication with a purpose.

Now let's talk about three other little words.

Paid. Owned. Earned.

Once upon at time, it was all about advertising, and all of our ads ran in paid media. Paid. You had to pay for the media space or time.

That simple media world is changing in interesting ways.

Now corporations, and other groups, like non-profits and governmental organizations, have a lot more ways to communicate – a lot more channels, a lot more options.

Once, when the media world was advertising dominant, we focused mainly on channels that were *paid* – things like newspaper and magazine ads, billboards, and commercials for TV and radio. All of that is still big business.

But now the playing field has grown as well.

Seen something you liked on YouTube? Maybe you were at a street fair and picked up a brochure that interested you, or maybe you picked up a free magazine and found that it was published by a drug store, or some hip marketer like Red Bull.

That sponsored magazine is *owned media.* The marketer owns it (a regular magazine, where you pay for an ad, is *paid* media – got it?).

Now what about that YouTube video that a friend told you about, or shared on Facebook? It might have been produced by a marketer, or it might have been someone's cat.

Either way, it's what we call *earned media*. It was so entertaining that it *earned* your attention.

Public relations focuses on earning media attention for their clients. It's one of their major responsibilities.

So… paid, owned, earned. You can remember that.

And, just as we remember that as a definition of how things are – wait a minute – it changes again.

One of our media friends told us we forgot one – **negotiated.** That's kind of a combination – we pay, but some of it is earned – sort of.

Look at the logos on NASCAR cars. Some of it is paid for with free tires and spark plugs, and maybe VIP tickets for key customers. And some of that deal was probably *negotiated.*

The point is, you need to understand that today's marketplace is a moving target. Yesterday's rate sheet is just the starting point for today's media thinking.

Now you're starting to understand why the media world we're heading into is getting a lot more interesting.

Best of all, smart new ideas can add value.

Six Little Words. One Big World.

OK, as you work to figure out how your future career fits into this changing world of strategic communication, you also need to stretch your mind to understand how big... and growing... and changing that world is.

TV commercials that turn into movies.

Careers that start in one place and grow into another.

This is the playing field you are entering. The game that you're getting ready to play is changing all the time.

Try to understand the range that's now available to you – and then focus on the fields that, on judgment, are the best fit for your strengths and your interests.

Got it? Good.

What is this StratThink Thing?

It's simply our word for *thinking strategically* – particularly about your own life. Every brand – including yours – does a better job when it has a strategy.

And we want you to get into the habit.

Thinking strategically helps you make better decisions.

It helps you stay on track as you work your way through a complicated world.

It gives you focus as you make your way through that multi-factor marketing and media environment we call real life.

Is every strategy the right strategy? No. And it's not unusual to discover that a combination of circumstances and things simply not going as well as we hoped will cause us to re-evaluate and re-strategize. It will be time for more StratThink.

Still, thinking strategically helps you get it right.

Hold that thought. Let's review what we just talked about.

Things To Do:

The purpose of this exercise is simple – Get your mind around today's range of career options in advertising, MarCom, and StratCom. Let's review.

- **How would you define MarCom and StratCom?**

- **Are there any areas right now that interest you?**

- **What are you going to do to find out a bit more?**

- **Memorize.** Write the six words, with your own definitions.

- **Categorize.** Write down the various types of MarCom. If you can't remember them all, review the section briefly.

Appendix: Two charts, courtesy *The Copy Workshop Workbook.*

1. **The MarCom Matrix**. A useful worksheet that can help you expand your idea into the different kinds of MarCom. You won't need it now. But one day soon…

2. **Media Evolution.** This chart shows how New Media and traditional media and MarCom techniques are evolving. As you look at types of media, it might be helpful.

MarCom Matrix Worksheet:

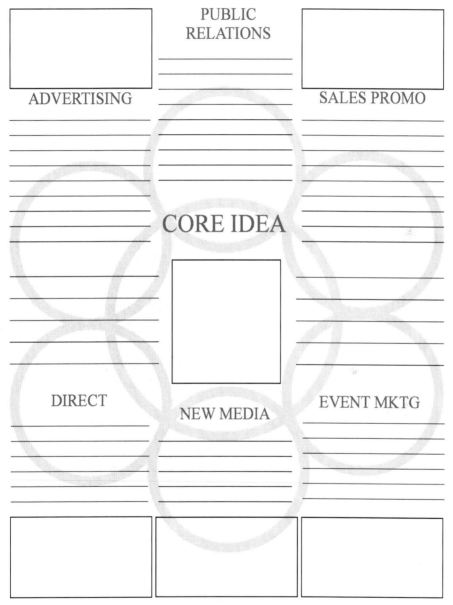

PUBLIC
RELATIONS

ADVERTISING

SALES PROMO

CORE IDEA

DIRECT

NEW MEDIA

EVENT MKTG

From The Copy Workshop Workbook

From left to right, you see how media forms are evolving – and the new techniques that are now necessary for success.

MEDIA

Traditional Media | Traditional Skills

Traditional Media	Traditional Skills
Basic Brand-Building	Environmental Strategy Design (Logistics)
Posters/Billboards	Clear and clever Local Customization (Directionals
Brochures/Catalog	Complete Information Good Organization Clear and Involving Copy Easy Ordering (if appropriate) 800#s and Order Forms
Print/Direct Response	Headline + Opening Sentence + Offer Generate Response Not Perceived as "Junk Mail"
Print/Brand Building	Reinforce Brand Values Build Awareness to Influence Purchase Decision
Radio	"Theater of the Mind" "Writer for the Ear"
Television	Audio/Visual Integration Involving "Cut through Clutter" Infomercials Long-form Video using Classic Direct Marketing Techniques

EVOLUTION

New Media and New Considerations also mean new Career opportunities.

New Media	New Considerations
Domain Names(s) **Online Presence**	Digital Strategy Engagement Memorability Relevance, "Stickiness" SEO - Google Ranking
Banner Ads **Video Boards**	Simple Animation Plus Click-through Response Animation Interactivity
Website	Menu/Navigation "Sticky" Involving E-Commerce (If appropriate) Database Capture
Email	Subject Header Initial Impression Click-through Response Not Perceived as "Spam"
Online Display	Generate Online Involvement SEO – Search Engine Optimization
Podcasts **HD Radio**	Podcast Programming Add Interactivity to Radio
Video/Viral	Generate Online Interest Turn Interest into Commerce Drive Traffic to site Infomercials Long-form Video (with New Interactive Capabilities)

13. Goal!

THERE'S AN OLD SAYING. *"When you don't know where you're going, any road will get you there."*

Even if your goals change, if you don't have some sort of target, you will always be kind of wondering and wandering.

OK, but two other things are probably true:

1. We really don't know exactly where we're going. Yet.

2. Things are real complicated. How can we really know?

Good points. There might even be a 3rd point.

3. There's really not that much I enjoy doing all the time. So why would I want to do that for the rest of my life?

Hey, nobody said it was going to be easy.

Maybe we don't yet have those "go-for-it" goals we'd all like to have, but you can still set some sensible short-term goals – like where you'd like to be making a living.

Or… What I'd like to be doing while I figure out what I'd like to be doing. See what I mean?

Setting realistic career goals, with realistic deadlines, is an important skill to develop.

Goal setting is also valuable for your own personal development and growth. Think about the bigger picture – like where you want to be in five years – and break down that seemingly insurmountable goal into smaller pieces.

That makes it a smaller goal that's easier to reach.

Plus, knowing where you might want to be in five years can come in handy when you decide where you might want to go for a few job interviews. Or a visit.

A Messy Business.

Remember, goal setting can be a messy business. You won't be right all the time and some goals may be out of reach.

There's one more problem. When we put that goal down in writing, in public, it can get weird.

If we said we'd do it and then didn't reach that goal, we can feel like some sort of failure. That stops a lot of people from setting goals and committing to them.

Well, get over it. Get used to it.

People in business fail all the time.

In fact, that's one of the ways we get smarter. Steve Jobs got fired before he came back and saved Apple. The lessons he learned made him a better person.

It's why evaluation is such an important part of the process.

Some ads don't work. Some brands fail.

Some companies go out of business – or change ownership. It happens. A lot.

Part of the excitement and the energy of our marketplace has a bit to do with the fact that when you try to do something new, well, you never know.

You may fail at some jobs. But a job isn't a career. As you build your career, you're going to have ups and downs.

Deal with it. When you think about it, that's part of finding your way into a career.

False Starts and Backtracks.

There may be false starts. You may have to backtrack.

You may end up somewhere totally different than where you thought you'd be. But that's part of building your brand.

Arm & Hammer Baking Soda thought they made something for baking. But the world changed. Now it deodorizes refrigerators. There may be a box in yours (or there should be).

Take a pencil. Write down some goals.
And remember, pencils have erasers. So lighten up.

A Few Other Thoughts:

As you're working to develop those short-term goals, here are some – possibly useful – thoughts.

- Look for work that needs doing. See any?

- How about some really short-term goals? How about this week? How about tomorrow?

- Got a Mission Statement? Why not? You can always change it. Give it some thought. What is your purpose? Don't know? Maybe that's your short-term goal. Find out.

- Looked at your *To Do list lately?

Sometimes we load it up with a lot of small stuff – start a new category – Big Stuff.

The First Step to Your Own Brand Strategy

Man is a strategic animal. We tend to operate more efficiently when we have a strategy.

A strategy, simply put, is an hypothesis about the best way to meet an objective – a goal.

When we know what that objective is, we're pretty good – all things considered – at getting there.

So… Got Strategy?

Actually, the first thing you have to ask is… Got Goal?

Things To Do:

OK, this is a big deal. But there really isn't a whole lot we can say about it. Start thinking more about your goals.
    Better yet, start doing something.
    See what happens.

- What do you think your goal is five years from now?

- Where would you like to be working?

- What would you like to be doing?

- What's your goal for the summer?

- What would you like to be learning?

- What experiences might benefit you?

- What are your goals for the weekend?

- Friday? Saturday? Sunday?

- What is your goal for next Monday?

14. You Are a Swiss Army Knife.

WE REPEAT. YOU ARE A SWISS ARMY KNIFE. We all are.
You know what I'm talking about, those multi-bladed beauties
with everything on them – from a plain old knife to a nail file
and corkscrew. And a toothpick hidden in the handle.

Later in this book, we're going to get serious
about some self-centered eval-
uation of your skills.

But let's start now.

Why don't you get out
one of those 3x5 cards?

Or maybe a 3-Up.

It's also a good time to
practice your printing.

The Best Blades Are...

OK, where do we stand?

As the subhead indicates, let's start with the good news.
What are the things you're kind of good at?

Now that doesn't always mean that's what you should do.
Hey, I was pretty good at math, but I didn't want to go into
that full time. Still, when we're doing some serious marketing
and lots of numbers hit the table, I'm still glad that's one of the
blades I can call on. Still fairly sharp.

Pick your three to five best. They may need to get bigger,
better, and sharper – but we're getting started.

As you work to sharpen your skills, it's not the worst thing
to start with something you're already fairly good at – just so
you don't hate it.

Middle of the Pack.

Sorry to say, my musical abilities were mediocre. I came to grips with that late in high school. I "played at it" during college, but I knew it wasn't going to be one of my "cutting edge skills."

I genuinely enjoyed music – thought I had a pretty good ear for what was good and what not so much. But I simply did not have the level of musical ability we expect from a professional.

Still, you never know. As time went on, I found myself doing more and more music production in the ad business.

And, for a few years, I was one-third of a music production company. Later on, one of my nicknames was "Jingles."

As a music producer, I wasn't bad. A shiny blade emerged from one not-so-sharp. My understanding of advertising, an ability to write lyrics, a growing amount of production experience, and good ears for a mix – they added up to real value.

Still, for the most part, I stayed away from the microphone. Well, maybe some announcing – if we didn't have a budget.

Years later, when I came out with a CD of my songs, we saluted my mediocre musical skills – and managed to keep expectations low.

Yes, that's me on the CD cover. *Can't Sing. Don't Care. Songs from the Hip.* Available from Amazon. We have plenty.

Blades That Need Work.

So… we can't be good at everything, but what blades would we like to be – or need to be – bigger, better, and sharper?

I'll tell you one blade I made better – finally. But it didn't get better until much later in life. Cooking. Grabbing a recipe and making dinner – it makes it a better world – better tasting, too – for me, and for those I'm with.

Then again, these days I can Google up a recipe – and that helps a lot.

A lot of us could do a bit more polishing on that get-more-exercise-every-day blade. You get the idea.

So, as you take a look at the smaller duller blades on your own Swiss Army knife, what would you like to make better?

Blades That Are Missing.

Take a look at the tools you're using. Are there a few more you should be getting good at? Are there some others that – a few years from now – might come in handy?

I'll tell you one category for all of us. Digital. Whether it's designing web sites – learning coding – getting fairly good at desktop publishing – producing your own blog or podcast… what blades can you add to your knife?

Scott's Swiss Army Knife.

This is a logo for my friend Scott Shellstrom. It's on his web site – www.shellstrom.com. Guess what he's good at?

Yes, pretty much all that stuff. Today, he makes a nice living using a bunch of nice sharp blades: design, fine art, film and video, photography,

Now all these blades and all of these skills didn't happen overnight. Scott worked hard, and at each job, he got better at something.

Sometimes it was producing film. He had a terrific career as an art director in New York and LA.

He hosted a cable TV show. Nice, but not quite as sharp as it needed to be. We learn.

If you lived in Cincinnati, you saw Scott in commercials for a few years – for one of the phone companies, I think. When he was starting out, he'd win dance contests.

Now he has a cool new speaker site – *Unleash Your Inner DaVinci.* Go Scott!

Strategy is about Choice.

Just because you're good at something doesn't mean that it's a career path. And, then again, sometimes it does.

So take a good look at your own Swiss Army Knife – keep sharpening. I hope it gets sharper and better over the years – with more and more blades that you can call your own.

Things To Do:

Let's review.

- **Right now, what are your "sharpest blades?"** (i.e., what are your strongest current skills?)

- **What are the blades the need some work?**

- **What are the blades that are missing? Which ones are you going to start on?** And finally…

- **How would you describe your ideal Swiss Army Knife ten years from now?** Give it a thought.

15. Career Gear Stage 2

IN THIS BOOK, Career Gear has three stages:

1. **Stage 1 is your initial Brand You Tools and Skills.** We start with some basics: Your Brand You Image, your 3-Up, and improved hand skills.

2. **Stage 2 emphasizes developing your "O.P."** That stands for your Online Presence. This includes: Resumé, initial Target Database, and what we'll call Brand Contact Points.

3. **Stage 3 is your Brand You Portfolio.** This will be a collection of relevant work aimed at your initial career goal. We'll get to that later.

For now, let's march through Stage 2: Résumé, Target Database, Online Presence, Brand Contact Points.

Your Résumé.

A résumé does more than list what you've done.

It also represents how you present yourself.

It should have clarity and purpose.

Have a few people look at your résumé and get suggestions. Look at a few others if you can. How do you stack up?

Your résumé is a summary of your knowledge, experiences, and skills. It's chock full of facts about you. The key is to develop the résumé that's right for you.

The One-Page Resumé.

In the beginning, try to keep it to one page. On that single page, you should be able to present – in clear and simple writing – why you are qualified for an entry-level job at a company in your target.

And since it's one of the first and most important ways your target will get to meet you, it's important.

It should be brief, pointed, dynamic, and well organized.

- Brief. One side of one sheet of paper.

- Pointed. It should note the experiences and skills tailored to your target and the position you're applying for.

- Dynamic. Select your words carefully. Use action verbs – they're the writer's best friend.

- Well Organized. There are two basic formats for résumés: Chronological and Functional. We'll add a third – personal.

The Chronological Résumé.

The most common format is to present information *in reverse chronological order,* with the most recent experience first.

A good outline for the résumé would be the following:

- **Contact Information:** Name, address, and phone number.

- **Objective:** A single, brief goal statement for that first job.

- **Education:** Name of school, Year, Degree, major/minor.

- **Special honors or achievements:** This may include Dean's lists, high GPA, leadership roles in organizations, or special commendations

- **Experiences and Employment:** Name/location of employer, and dates of employment. Job title and responsibilities.

If possible, include brief descriptions of those jobs that reflect well on you and relate to your objective or what you believe fits well with your employer's need.

If you happen to have paid for a large percentage of your college costs, you may even want to state that in an appropriate way, since this will reflect well on you. (If all you've got is a big student debt, skip it.)

If appropriate, you may want to break your experiences or employment out into two sections:

- Related Experience

- Additional employment.

- Again, think about your target.

- Activities and Interests. If it's interesting, include brief lists or descriptions of activities that personalize you and reflect on how you might fit with the company.

- References: Generally, avoid listing references on a one-page résumé; However, if you have strong references who have agreed to support you, then you should seriously consider using a separate piece of paper to highlight them. Include name, title, address, and phone number for each reference. And you should always make certain your references agree in advance to your request.

Even though the most common format is to present information in reverse chronological order, if there's something in your background that should be brought to the attention of the company you can move it to the front.

For example, if you're applying to an international firm and you've spent a significant amount of time abroad with relevant language skills – get that information up front.

The Functional Résumé.

The functional résumé is based on skills rather than chronology. It is meant to highlight the match between your skill set and what the employer needs.

For the most part, it follows the chronological résumé format:

- **Contact Information**

- **Objective**

- **Education**

- **Experiences**

- **Skills.** Expand this section. Note skills you've gained from previous experiences or employment that relate to those desired by the employer.

    Add more than one Skills section if appropriate. For example, you might title one section, "Organizational Skills." And another "Software Skills."

    Don't over-use the "skills" word. For example, a subhead that said "Sales Experience," would be appropriate – not "Sales Skills."

The Personal Résumé

We don't recommend this for everyone, but sometimes it's appropriate to modify the format to project a unique personality.

Here is a unique and memorable résumé that Maxine Paetro featured in her job-hunting classic, *How to Put Your Book Together and Get a Job in Advertising.*

This résumé was unique. And it worked. Take a look

A Unique and Memorable Résumé.

June to Present. Part-time chauffeur/word processor for New York consulting firm specializing in non-profit organizations.

- Transport President to and from appointments.

- Edit and type staff associates' fundraising proposals.

- Deliver and recover Blanche (President's cat) to and from vet.

- Claim President's fur from furrier.

- Bring in President's pearls for repair.

June to February – Mr. B__, New York. Live-in companion/cook to 90-year-old man.

- Accompanied Mr. B__ on walks through United Nations Park. Often stopped to see Moon Rock.

- Coordinated and prepared Sunday lasagna luncheons.

- Initiated subscription to *New York Times* large print edition.

September to May – New York. Au pair for divorce lawyer and her 12-year-old son.

- Laundered their dirty clothing.

- Washed their filthy dishes.

- Cleaned their stinking kitchen.

- Prepared their wretched meals.

- Never complained once.

Get the idea? On one level, these experiences were ordinary – they were commodities on the low-end of the job market.

But this person made them extraordinary.

This person communicated life lessons and more.

This little résumé was a window into the quality of the person who had those experiences.

And it demonstrated she could flat-out write.

This is an outstanding example of what a brand personality can do to add value.

The actual jobs were ordinary.

The presentation made them *extraordinary.*

Look at your growing list of experiences through the lens of your own brand personality. Try to reflect that in your resumé.

Do that and you're beginning to position yourself in the crowded job marketplace.

Target Database

Do you have a Contact/Address program?

How "robust" is it?

If it's just the Contact/Address list on your mobile phone, you need to get something better. And the sooner you start, the less re-inputting and updating you'll have to do.

So, what program? We're not sure.

We use Macs – mostly – and early on there was really only one choice – FileMaker – so we use that. It's fine, and we need something pretty complicated, with linking databases, and inventory, and stuff like that.

But today, there are a lot of programs – many are less expensive and will do just fine. I guess I'd say read the reviews and choose one. But you absolutely do need one.

Here's what you'll need to be able to do:

1. **List (and Search)** – Names, Addresses, Phone Numbers, and email addresses.

2. **Add notes for other useful information** – like when your uncle mentioned a friend who owns a sports marketing company, or a person you knew casually from high school who now works where you'd like to work. Yes!

3. **Your own personal codes.** For the holidays, we send out delicious cakes from Racine. Kringles! We have a set of codes: Kringle1, Kringle2, Kringle3, Bringle (for a business address – we need a different address configuration), and Dringle (when they live close by and we deliver them).

You'll develop your own codes as years go by. Let's say you go to Western Michigan – in some part of the database, put your chosen code WM, or Western Michigan, or UWM – whatever – but pick one! (You'll find that if you alternate between "U of" and "University of" you're going to run into problems down the road.) You might even want to write down a short list of those codes.

4. **Emailing capabilities.** If possible, you want to be able to send out email blasts. Not a lot – but something. And, you'll find that as your list starts to grow, you'll have other things to deal with. Firewalls. Limits on the number of emails you can send out. These are things you'll deal with down the road. You may also find that you'll want to send out mailings in real mail. Not so much right now – but for wedding invitations (Hey, it could happen), or announcements of your brand new job (Yay!). You'll be glad you got started with a solid-up-to-date and easy-to-use database.

Business Cards.

You're going to start to collect them. What do you do?

Sometimes they're important and valuable, and often they are just the debris of 21st Century life. It's like you were somewhere and somebody gave you a card. Darned if you can remember anything else about it.

What about one of those scan the card gizmos? If you're going into something where this could be important – like sales – look into it.

Some of these are services that want you to pay a monthly fee for all eternity. My instincts are to take a pass on something like that.

But the key is that you do *something* – and keep on it.

For a start, get a box to hold 'em. You'll be surprised how quickly they fill up. Try to keep track of the important ones.

Your "O.P." Your Online Presence.

You already have a bit of an O.P., right? We're guessing it's Facebook and a few other bits and pieces of social media.

For a start, you need to do three things.

1. **Input a solid LinkedIn profile – with a good photo.** There might not be much to it – yet – but let's have something nice and professional.

2. **Get your URL.** You might not be putting up a site yet, but let's think ahead. Try for your name. Your name with a dash if your name is already taken. Perhaps something else from your Brand You personality. Your name plus something from your Brand You personality. You want a .com (that's dot.com) if possible. Though .net and some of the others aren't bad. More on this in a bit.

3. **Clean-up your Facebook profile.** Those party pictures. The funny stuff your friends sent you. Get 'em off the site. It's fine to have your own folder with stuff that makes you smile. And – if you want to send – privately – things that make you laugh out loud because they're outrageous, hey, we never said everything has to be on the straight and narrow. But – in public where everyone and anyone can see it – straight and narrow is *exactly* what you want.

Now, a bit more about that URL/domain name.

Getting Your Domain Name.

Step 1. Secure a domain name. While there are plenty of free website providers out there to host your online portfolio, you won't come off as truly professional in the online space without a dedicated domain name.

For example, johndoe.com is much more professional than mypowermall2.com/johndoe/portfolio. Most of the URL providers have nice user-friendly sites – like Network Solutions (the original), or GoDaddy – despite advertising that was not to my taste. Pretty much any of the others – they're fine.

Just check to see that their low-price doesn't come with other stuff attached – like mandatory hosting fees.

Get that URL now! You might not be using it yet, but reserving and owning a domain name is inexpensive and you'll be glad you did it. Get a few if you can – it's still a bargain.

Step 2. Find a provider to host your website. This is optional. You really might not be ready. When you do, if you're not going to be a site designer yourself, and you don't have access to someone good and inexpensive, give some preference to a hosting site that includes a site builder. These providers allow you to create a website, including an online portfolio, from a collection of templates and layouts you can customize to meet your needs. I used MacWeb for my Czech site - worked fine.

Step 3. Build your website. Even though, at this stage you'll be using the site primarily as a platform for a portfolio, it's best to create the following:

- A Home page

- An About page

- At least one Portfolio page. If you have work in various media, you might want more than one.

- A dedicated page to testimonials might be a good idea. If your name is Jane, call it We Like Jane.

If your name isn't Jane, call it something else.

- Additional pages add to your professionalism.

Step 4. Learn how to update your site yourself, if possible.

Step 5. Get SEO cues imbedded in your site. Your name, and desired career area. Other cues that reinforce your brand.

Step 6. Put your Web address on other Brand Contact Points – like your 3-Up.

Step 7 & Beyond. What areas do you need to improve? Graphics? Are you ready for video yet? (You might want to start learning.)

Your Brand Contact Points.

So, what happens when somebody Googles your name?

For a start, we're assuming that your LinkedIn profile and your Facebook page will show up.

Now, what else can we do that makes sense?

Getting SEO (Search Engine Optimization) cues onto your website is a sensible next step. Here's a checklist:

Your "OP," Online Presence:

    ❏ Personal URL

    ❏ Website

    ❏ Facebook page.

    ❏ LinkedIn profile.

    ❏ Other Social Media (pick the ones that work for you):
        Twitter
        Instagram
        Pinterest

SnapChat,

_____

_____

❏ Set up a YouTube account. Post relevant Videos.

❏ Ready for a blog or podcast yet? Probably not. But you might want to start thinking about it. And learning.

OK, that's a good start.

Things To Do:

How many of the things in this chapter have you accomplished so far? Check them off when done. This may take a while. Don't worry, just keep moving forward.

❏ **Résumé written.**

❏ **I now have a box for business cards.**

❏ **The target market database program I have chosen is**

_____.

❏ **My target market database program is up and running.**

❏ **Domain name selected and purchased.**

❏ **Web host selected.**

❏ **Web site designed.**

❏ **Web site up and running with SEO cues.**

❏ **LinkedIn profile – with appropriate photo.**

❏ **Facebook Page – without inappropriate photos.**

❏ **Other Additions to my "O.P."**

    ❏ **Twitter Account w. activity.**

    ❏ **Instagram.**

    ❏ **Pinterest.**

    ❏ **Snap Chat.**

    ❏ **YouTube Account opened.**

And... from your *To Do: list...

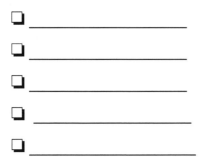

    ❏ _____

    ❏ _____

    ❏ _____

    ❏ _____

    ❏ _____

16. Four Big Ideas:
Shaping The 21ˢᵗ Century.

FOUR BIG IDEAS – some over 100 years old – are having an impact on your economic future. Those four big thinkers are:

- **Joseph Schumpeter** (1883-1950) Austrian economist.

- **Gordon Moore** (1929) American computer genius

- **Marshall McLuhan** (1911-1980) Canadian media guru

- **Paul Romer** (1955) American economist and entrepreneur.

    Now let's wrap our heads around their four big ideas.

Schumpeter & Creative Destruction.

Joseph Schumpeter, was an Austrian economist and political scientist. In 1919, he briefly served as Austria's Finance Minister.

In 1932, he left Austria for good and became a professor at Harvard University, where he remained until the end of his career. He became a US citizen in 1939.

He was one of the most influential economists of the 20th Century. The reason we still pay attention to him in the 21st

Century is a concept he popularized *"Creative Destruction."*

What is that? It's something we live with every day – and something that will concern you in your search for the right career.

It was Schumpeter's observation that, as capitalism creates new businesses opportunities, it also destroys existing ones.

That cool new camera on your mobile phone helped wipe out a huge company – Kodak. We don't need much photo film anymore do we?

As the automobile industry was created, the horse and buggy industry had to change or die. Maybe both.

This cycle of change is a reality you must understand. For example, your career may begin with a growing company that's creating exciting new opportunities.

Then, ten years later, a new way of doing business, or maybe a whole new industry, or simply another new idea, could change things almost overnight.

Some companies can last a century. Others can't.

That's creative destruction at work. We'll come back to this important thought when we look at the modern marketplace.

Moore's Law. Gordon Moore's Really Good Guess.

He was a co-founder of Intel – one of the world's major manufacturers of computer chips - semiconductors.

In 1965, he was asked by *Electronics Magazine* to predict what was going to happen in the semiconductor industry over the next ten years. Moore observed that integrated circuit capacity doubled approximately every year, and he speculated this would continue.

In 1975, he revised his forecast rate to approximately every two years.

This good guess became known as *"Moore's Law."*

A related factor is a dramatic decrease in relative cost. Your computers get better – and they get cheaper!

A rough rule of thumb emerged.

Every eighteen months, computer capacity doubled and the cost of that capacity was cut in half. Wow!

You see the effect of Moore's Law in the computer on your desk, the phone in your pocket or purse, and the growing digital capability in almost everything around us.

Even though chip technology is now down to almost the molecular level, Gordon Moore's "best guess" still seems to be in operation.

What does this mean for us? It means that as we try to see the future, we can be confident that our crystal ball will be operating with increasing digital capability and lower costs.

That's Moore's Law at work.

Marshall McLuhan. Welcome to the Revolution.

There's a humorous observation attributed to San Francisco ad legend Howard Gossage, *"We don't know who discovered water, but we're pretty sure it wasn't a fish."*

That reminds us that we're not always aware of the water we're swimming in. Media is one of those things we swim in. When the media we swim in changes, we change.

And our world changes. One of McLuhan's earliest books was *The Gutenberg Galaxy.* He observed that when books became commonplace – thanks to Gutenberg's invention of printing from moveable type – the world changed.

Society became literate. No longer were "truth" and knowledge owned by the rich and a priestly class.

Now the Bible could be printed and then read in the

people's language. New thoughts could now be easily printed, distributed, and shared with everyone.

It was no accident that the invention of the printing press was followed closely by The Reformation, the Thirty Years War, and the American Revolution.

Let's remember that "The First American," Ben Franklin – was a printer. Media – the printing press – with writings like Thomas Paine's *Common Sense*, and the Declaration of Independence itself was the driving force of our Revolution.

McLuhan showed us how a change in media changes society. From FDR's "Fireside Chats" on radio, through the birth and growth of TV – from a small black and white box flickering in the living room corner, to a giant color screen dominating our home environment… we swim in new media environments all the time. And, as a result, our world changes.

Now the computer has changed it again. We don't just read and watch and listen. We search. We share.

And… we *broadcast!* How many of you have posted something on YouTube? In your new career, you may create something new with a desktop publishing program, an audio/video editing program – or maybe Garage Band! *BrandYouTV!*

Now, as growing computer capability (Thank You, Moore's Law) roars through our changing economy (Watch Out! It's Creative Destruction!!), our new wired-together media world – the "Global Village" that McLuhan predicted – is here.

Paul Romer & The Economic Power of Ideas.

His father was governor of Colorado. He received degrees in math and economics at the University of Chicago and brought some important new insights to the field of economics – the big idea that knowledge and ideas themselves have become a powerful new force in our modern economy.

Those who want to keep you from understanding it call it *endogenous growth theory.*

Huh? It's actually a wonderful big idea – the thought that thinking itself has great positive economic value.

It's the idea that human capital, innovation, and knowledge are, in themselves, very significant contributors to our economic growth.

Romer observes that our economy is more and more being driven by *good ideas!* That's why not every job goes to the lowest wage sector of the economy – or the cheapest country.

It means that ideas count. And it means that one of the reasons our future might be a bit brighter than some think is that new ideas have the power to make things better.

Whether it's new software, new economic models, a new hit song, or a new idea that makes us healthier and happier, it's where a lot of future economic growth is going to come from.

And that's good news for people who like to think.

Today, Paul alternates between being a professor at New York University (he moved there from Stanford) and being an entrepreneur. In 2001, he took time off to develop a startup – Aplia – which developed online homework to help students learn more effectively.

Romer's idea is powerful – for all of us. In 1997, he was named one of America's 25 most influential people by *Time.* He has also received many other awards.

But the biggest reward is the thought that our lives will be enriched by better ideas. Doesn't that sound nice?

Ideas For the Future.

We don't know all that the 21st Century will bring.

But we do know that those four big ideas will be part of it.

So as you make your way into a future that's hard to know exactly, you can be confident that these four underlying forces will be a part of that future:

- **Creative Destruction.** As new ideas emerge, old ones go.

- **Moore's Law.** This explains the growing availability and use of ever-more-economical computer processing.

- **Media Evolution** is revolutionizing our society as the shift to digital continues.

- **The Power of Ideas.** Good ideas will continue to generate economic growth in a new and changing world.

Hold those thoughts. All four of them. Together, they're going to impact the world that you're getting ready for.

Things To Do/Discussion Topics:

There are some big thoughts here. (No kidding.) Let's give them just a little more thought. They deserve it.

- **Creative Destruction.** In your personal experience, can you name anyone hurt by "creative destruction?"

- When you think of the "creative" part, what new companies come to mind?

- When you think of "destruction," what comes to mind?

- In the future (next 5-10 years) what businesses do you think will be created? What will "mature" or be destroyed?

- **Moore's Law.** In your personal experience, what things in your life have been affected by Moore's Law?

- In the future, what things do you think will come into your life with a major boost from Moore's Law?

- **McLuhan's Thoughts on Media & Society.** In your personal experience, how is your life and behavior being affected by the media you use? And the way you use it.

- In the future, how do you think your media behavior will change?

- What else do you think will be affected by media evolution?0

- **The Power of Ideas.** In your personal experience, what new ideas have affected your life?

- In the future, what might be some opportunities for new ideas to make things better?

17. Making Connections & Building Your Database.

IS YOUR DATABASE UP AND RUNNING? Let's give it an initial workout. Here's what we're going to do.

Getting Organized.

- **Update your database.** Establish three categories:
  <u>Family</u> and two kinds of friends.
  <u>HS</u> – High School – and whatever code you want to use for the university. If there's a third kind of friend - add a new code for that as well.

- **Add two more levels to your database:**
  <u>FamilyR</u> – for relatives who are out of town.
  <u>Prof</u> – after your University code add the word Prof to any instructors you want to remember – and who might want to remember you.

- **Start a small text file.** Call it Database Code – whatever you want. List categories and codes. Set up your own coding system. It's your database – do what you want.

- **Start a newsletter.** You're going to send it in a bit. If this is Fall Semester, it's going to be a holiday note. If it's Spring Semester, you'll write about your upcoming summer – you'll tell us what you'll be doing and how to stay in touch with you. If it's none of the above, it's time to write a short "Hello" piece titled "Welcome to My Database."

- **Fill in the blanks on your database.** You're probably missing email addresses, university addresses of high school friends who are going to school somewhere else (you're going to be happy you took the time to stay in touch), and updated information on out-of-town relatives (your parents can probably help there).

- **Email attachments.** Learn how your email attachment works in your database program. Can you send PDFs? Can you send them with live links? Do graphics show up in the document or as an attachment? Can you imbed photos? If it's a one-page newsletter, how will the database program handle it?

Getting in Touch. Staying in Touch.

The Obama presidential campaign did lots of testing to see which email headline would perform best. One of the very best performing subject lines was... Hey!

Do a simple Contact e-mail that tells the recipient "Welcome to My Database." Let them know you want to stay in touch and ask if you have all the right info. If there's a friend of a friend – or a relative of a relative – missing from that database, ask for the information.

Provide your information – and realize that – from year to year – university address information comes and goes. Your email, mobile phone number, and – for a while – your home address will stay the same.

If there's any additional personal stuff, either add a PS – or make each email a bit more of a custom job. Up to you.

And – if you're already in pretty good shape with your personal database – let's see how we can make it better.

How about one more category? Career.

Not a lot of entries yet?

Hey, you're just getting started.

Things To Do:

How many of the things in this chapter have you accomplished so far? Check them off when done. This may take a while. Don't worry – just keep moving forward.

❏ Database program up and running.

❏ Database updated with Family and Friends.

❏ Initial database categories and codes established.

❏ "Welcome to my database." Contact email created.

❏ Initial update email sent out.

❏ Short newsletter created w. at least one imbedded photo (Holiday or Summer version).

❏ Newsletter sent.

❏ Optional – "Hey!" update email.

18. Team Up!

WORKING ALONE. That's what's involved in much of schoolwork. Athletics often involves playing on a team, but in school, you're pretty much on your own.

That's not a bad thing. For now. We each learn at our own speed – and what it takes to master the material is often something we have to do alone.

However, with many of the jobs waiting for you out there – particularly in marketing and communication – the final "product" is usually the result of collaborative effort.

Correction. Make that "almost always."

So, even though "Teamwork 101" probably isn't offered in the course catalog, getting better at working with others should start to be one of your objectives – even if you already think you're pretty good at it.

For example, how's your "Emotional IQ?"

Your Emotional IQ.

In today's workplace, you'll be judged not just for technical skills and how smart you are – but by how well you handle the modern work environment.

That means knowing how to work with others.

We need to develop *"emotional intelligence."*

What is that? Good question. It means you need the right emotional habits and control as well as technical skills.

Today, it takes more than those technical abilities to succeed in the workplace.

It might not affect getting your first job, but it can have a huge impact on keeping that job – and getting promoted.

So let's get a little smarter about Emotional IQ.

Where's my Wikipedia?

Four Kinds of Emotional IQ.

What are these abilities? Wiki says there are four types of skills:

- **Perceiving emotions** – this is the ability to detect and decipher emotions in faces, voices, behaviors, and social cues. It includes the ability to identify our own emotions. This is a core aspect of emotional intelligence, as it makes all other emotional information processing possible.

- **Using emotions** – this is the ability to harness your emotions and use them for a productive purpose, such as problem-solving, thinking, and providing appropriate emotional support for someone else. An emotionally intelligent person is able to use his or her emotions and changing moods productively to fit the task at hand.

- **Understanding emotions** – this is the ability to comprehend emotion in others and ourselves and appreciate the complexity. Understanding emotions includes the ability to be sensitive to slight emotional variations, and recognize and describe how emotions can change over time.

- **Managing emotions** – this is the ability to regulate emotions in both ourselves and others. An emotionally intelligent person can harness emotions, even negative ones, and manage them to achieve intended goals.

As you can see, these are four aspects of one big thing. And that one big thing is a major determinant of how well we work as part of a group.

Giving Credit. Sharing Credit.

One of the key aspects in group dynamics is the fact that people wish to be valued. For some, this is a driving need, others are more relaxed about the whole thing.

You, however, should have a firm and consistent standard – give credit where credit is due. Sometimes, even when it isn't. (You be the judge on that – some people do a ton of work with no need for too many compliments – others seem to need praise for putting a dish in the sink.)

In team projects, this can be a big deal. Most of us know that collaboration is part of the business, and, when we look at your portfolio, we're OK when you tell us who did what.

On the other hand, if you try to take *all* of the credit, we might start to get a bit suspicious.

Sad to say, people taking credit for others' work is happens at every level of just about every business.

It is almost certain that you will run into it – and you will probably be unhappy about it – particularly if it's your work that someone else takes credit for.

Look at it this way, now you know who you don't want to work with in the future. Valuable information.

So… if you've collaborated on a project, credit those you worked with. Not only is it the right thing to do, it also shows that you know how to play on a team.

Learn to Be #2 on a Good Idea.

This is, quite frankly, one of the secrets to my modest success. I've been associated with a lot of "work that worked."

Quite a bit, actually.

Some of those ideas started out as mine – many others came from the smart, good-looking people I worked with.

Sometimes you see everyone jockeying for *their* idea – and sometimes another idea in the room is terrific! I was often lucky enough to be the creative in charge, so I could just get behind that good idea as part of doing my job. But…

Earlier in my career, it was different. Either I'd chime up in the meeting and let it be known I thought that was a pretty good idea. Or, if it came to me later, I'd just tell the person with the idea, "Hey, that's terrific! Can I help?"

Generally, people are pleased to get a bit of affirmation and a bit of help – though don't be surprised if they're surprised. (If they'd rather keep it to themselves, that is their perogative.)

I've also often seen that one good idea is just a step on the road to an even better idea. But you have to start somewhere.

Next time you're in a group project and someone else has an idea you like… go public and see what happens.

Becoming Emotionally Smarter.

Emotional IQ can be improved. If we try, we really can get better at balancing priorities, keeping our temper, and paying more attention to others. But you do have to work at it.

Many of our emotional habits were established early in life. Here's the general approach:

- Identify areas where you can become emotionally smarter. We bet you know them already.

- Practice new responses. If there's someone who knows you pretty well, that person might help you identify the new responses to work on.

- Find a role model with habits you admire – try to copy them. You will still be you, but all of us could use a bit of a software upgrade, right?

- Develop a basic understanding of body language. Then use the things you've learned. Think about your posture and your behavior. Unfold those arms.

Many school activities can be good ways of developing your emotional competencies – both as a leader and as a team member. In each role, coach yourself to improve.

Want to be a better leader? Ask for feedback – let them know you want to hear. You won't always like what you hear – and not all of it will be useful – but, over time, you'll improve.

You can become a better team member just by making it a conscious goal in every meeting. Soon, it will be a habit.

You can do this! Emotional IQ is a combination of learned behaviors and our own sense of empathy toward our fellow human beings.

Some of us will be better than others. But that's sort of true about everything, isn't it? The big point is you really can change and improve these things – and now is the right time to do it.

Changing can be hard work. After all, you're dismantling an old habit and building a new one. Old habits die hard.

But it's a genuine opportunity. Think about it.

In a market dominated by change, one thing you really can change is *you*.

Improving Your Collaboration.

A lot of work in modern firms involves "cross-functional" teams. "Cross-functional" simply means a group of people with different abilities – different functional expertise working together to achieve a common goal.

For example, a team could have a market researcher, an account manager, copywriter, designer, production person, and project manager – all working together.

This is different from most group projects in college, but not the AAF/NSAC competition. They do try to replicate this traditional ad agency style of organization. It's one reason to try it, even if you're not going into advertising.

People working on cross-functional teams must be able to communicate smoothly even when everyone has a totally different role. It's how a lot of the world outside works.

Figuring out what you're good at is part of it.

Working with others who are good at what they do is a big part of it. The final key? Having a good time doing it!

In the 21ˢᵗ Century, business is a team sport.

You need to be someone others want to have on their team·

Things To Do:

We'd like to suggest you seek out additional team opportunities. We know that you probably have a fairly full schedule already. But here are some things you can do:

- **Become more aware.** Seriously. When you're working in a group, simply become more conscious of what's going on. If you're a team member, look for ways to be better at it. When you're the leader, maybe let them know you're trying to work on your leadership skills. Ask for feedback.

- **Do your own Emotional IQ inventory**. Think about it. Write down things you think you're OK with – and things where you probably need to do a bit more work. Bet you get better at what you want to improve.

- **Read about body language.** Here's an example…
  "A person sitting until the back of his/her chair, leans forward with his/her head nodding along with the discussion implies that he/she is open, relaxed and generally ready to listen. On the other hand, a person who has his/her legs and arms crossed with the foot kicking slightly implies that he/she is feeling impatient and emotionally detached from the discussion." [From Wikipedia.]

  Interesting, isn't it? Find out more.
  Then, apply what you've learned.

IV. Getting Your Career in Gear.

THESE FOUR SYMBOLS are the Chinese Celestial Animals. They represent North, South, East, and West. Each also stands for one of the four stages in our Career Strategy:

- *The Tiger (West) represents understanding yourself as a brand.* It involves knowing your strong points, your weak points, your best opportunities, and areas where you might want to do a little work.

- *The Phoenix (South) represents understanding the market.* He is in a constant state of rebirth. Remember our discussion of Schumpeter and "Creative Destruction?" This is a key reality of today's marketplace – and you want to aim for the growth part of this natural cycle of change. Right?

- *The Turtle (North) is about increasing your market value.* With slow steady steps, he protects and strengthens. He is the symbol of increasing your own abilities and advantages.

- *The Dragon (East) represents taking yourself to market.* He can bring you inspiration, wealth, and great good fortune as you strive toward your goal. Let's get started.

19. Understand Yourself as a Brand.

HOW WELL DO WE KNOW OURSELVES? In some ways, very well. We know how tall we are, the color of our hair, and how we look in the mirror.

Only, when you think about it, the mirror shows it to us backwards! What else are we missing?

For a start, let's take another look at who we are, with particular attention to those strengths that might help us succeed in today's marketplace.

Personal Inventory I: Unique vs. Commodity.

A personal inventory is an essential step in building Brand You! You need to take an objective look at your strengths, your weaknesses, and your personality.

We also need to realize that some of the things about us – like the sports teams we root for, and the degree we're going to receive from our university when we graduate, are *commodities*.

Think about it. They're kind of similar for everyone who has one. Yes, you're working hard for it – and it's important. But realize that when the marketplace looks at your hard-won degree, it's going to look pretty much the same as all the other hard-won degrees – not only from your university or college, but kind of all of them.

We need to focus on the things that make you special.

"The Brand Called You."

That was the title of the cover story in the very first issue of *Fast Company* magazine. It was written by the very cool marketing guru Tom Peters. You can still read the whole thing at

Here's some of what he had to say: *"Regardless of age, regardless of position, regardless of the business we happen to be in, all of us need to understand the importance of branding.*

"We are CEOs of our own companies: Me, Inc. To be in business today, our most important job is to be head marketer for the brand called You."

So, congratulations on your promotion to head marketer of Brand You! Peters has more to say…

"You're every bit as much a brand as Nike, Coke, Pepsi, or the Body Shop. To start thinking like your own favorite brand manager, ask yourself the same question the brand managers at Nike, Coke, Pepsi, or the Body Shop ask themselves:

"What is it that my product or service does that makes it different?" That is the question we want to answer first.

What makes us unique – and not a commodity?

Personal Inventory II: T.I.G.E.R.

When we first developed this program as part of the Careers Section of *Advertising & The Business of Brands*, Professor Jim Marra of Temple University put together this personal inventory system with easy-to-remember letters. It works nicely.

T = Talents.
I = Interests
G = Goals
E = Experiences
R = Resources.

Now, you might want to get out a notebook or note pad for this next section. Because, as we work our way through the various categories, there are going to be some things about you that you'll want to write down.

Some will be obvious. But some others might be just a bit surprising. So get out that notebook – and it's a good time to practice your handwriting.

Talents. For a Start, What Are You Good At?

Let's take a look at your talents. Remember, just because you happen to be good at it, doesn't mean you want to do it for the rest of your life.

Bruce, your hard-working author, was good at math. But he still didn't want to be a full time accountant. (The math did help when he had to work his way through piles of marketing data.)

Everyone's good at something. What about you?

What have you been praised for? What have your parents, friends, and teachers told you that you're good at?

In short, what are your talents and skills?

Let's start that T.I.G.E.R. worksheet.

What do you have under talents? Take your time.

Writing? Math? Leading and organizing people?

How about presenting in front of groups?

Are you a problem-solver? It's not just school work.

What are those things you do well? What do you think are your special and unique talents? Write down your favorite.

Is that something you'd like to keep doing?

You might want to think of two columns in your "T" for Talent listing. On one side, things you're good at – and like to do. And on the other side, things you might be good at, but don't like to do – like washing dishes.

You get the idea. Write 'em down.

An Interest Inventory.

Next on our list is "I for Interests." In many cases, our talents are related to our interests. After all, chances are, you're a bit talented in things that interest you.

Of course, this isn't totally true. We can have lots of interest in music or sports without the talent to do it professionally.

So get out that note pad and let's identify your interests.

For example, Craig liked cars. He knew how they worked, and he knew how to fix them.

When Craig prepared his copywriting portfolio, it was probably no surprise that the ads about automobiles were the best in his book.

Craig discovered, and was discovered by, agencies that worked in the "automotive aftermarket." These are companies that market all the things you need to keep a car running.

Craig combined his talent as a writer with his car-repairing hobby and became an award-winning copywriter in the field of automotive aftermarket advertising.

Thirty years later, he's still doing it.

But now he makes enough to pay others to change his oil.

List your interests. It might be a clue.

From Hobby to Profession.

Don't forget to list your hobbies. It might be another clue.

No kidding.

I have a nephew, Steve. He was into baseball cards. He'd go get autographs, and collect them, and put them in order, and go to the shows, and all that. His father and I would look at all those boxes of cards and roll our eyes.

Today, you can see Steve on one of those reality TV shows. He's an "authenticator" in sports memorabilia, and it looks like he's turned his hobby into a nice career. A very nice career.

Now when Steve pulls into the driveway in his BMW with his wife and kids, his dad and I smile. We nod, and act like we knew it all along. Hey, you never know.

Write down those things that interest you. And maybe you'll want to know more. For example, your favorite hobby probably has an industry that supports some form of advertising – and maybe a magazine. A website for sure.

Do you know anything about the company that makes your favorite product – or provides a service aligned with your favorite hobby? Maybe you should.

Is there an industry trade association? What's on the web site? Identify your interests, and compare them to that list of talents. They tend to go together.

Here's one more clue – and it's from an actual genius – Buckminster Fuller. He was asked by a student how to know what it is you should do. Fuller observed that you can know the answer by tracing your own history and identifying what it is that you did – and continued to do – when others (parents, friends, teachers) weren't telling you what to do. Thanks, Bucky.

Jot them down on that note pad.

G = Goals. You Can Have More Than One.

We all need goals. And, when you think about it, goals are one of the things that differentiate marketers – and their brands.

Your goal may be simple. Like *"Get a job that doesn't suck."* Though we think you'll be happier with a goal that includes what you do want – not just what you don't want to do.

And you can have more than one goal.

Like short term and long term.

For example, a short-term goal might be to go find a job in Portland, Oregon – and enjoy the outdoor activities. A long-term goal might be – work in sports marketing – with an emphasis on outdoor activities.

What's a BHAG?

OK, you don't necessarily need to have one – but you should know what that is – because a lot of companies have them.

BHAG stands for – are you ready?

Big Hairy Audacious Goal. It was an idea conceptualized in the book, *"Built to Last: Successful Habits of Visionary Companies"* by James Collins and Jerry Porras. A BHAG is a long-term goal that changes the very nature of a business' existence.

You'll find a lot of them at the high-tech and software companies in Silicon Valley and the San Francisco startups. You might want one as well.

At Leo Burnett, a very successful ad agency, their logo was a hand reaching for the stars with this slogan:

"When you reach for the stars you may not quite get one, but you won't come up with a handful of mud either."

Give it a thought.

Are You Experienced?

Most potential employers are more interested in your experiences than your interests. They want to know where you've worked and what you've done.

As you look at your note pad, give a thought to what you've learned so far. Even though you're young, you've probably had relevant experiences – experiences that count.

Even entry-level jobs can be very educational. Dealing with the public – learning what it takes to put in a full day's work – and accumulating a few early life lessons… it all adds up.

Ideally, some of those experiences will be connected with your talents and interests. It stands to reason.

You have a talent for something because you're interested. Then you actualize that talent,. That results in your experiences.

Now is the time to list them. If you feel they're in short supply, well, that tells you something right there.

Remember, you still have a bit of time to get your "brand" in shape for the marketplace. You might want to think about the kinds of experiences you'd like to add.-

Look at your experiences. See anything?

Any clues to your brand personality?

OK, one more letter to go.

R = Resources.

Strategy is the search for advantage in the marketplace. Let's see if we can identify some of your initial advantages.

Your first two resources are education and experience.

Your other main resource is the human connection.

Simply put, who do you know? And who do they know?

For the most part, your resources will consist of your friends and relatives – and their friends and relatives.

In fact, you might want to get out a fresh sheet for the note pad, and think about how you might update that database you set up. Because some of your major resources are, quite simply, friends and family.

"Don't Send Nobody Nobody Sent."

That's a saying they have in Chicago. Who you know counts.

Is this fair? Not particularly.

But, in many ways, in many circumstances, it's simply the way things work. Summer internships. Entry-level jobs. An interview. Someone who knows someone.

In many cases, resources can make the critical difference.

Melissa's dad called a friend he knew. The friend scheduled an interview. A job had just opened up. Melissa got the job.

She got the job on her merits. But she got the interview on her relationships. Again, resources can make the difference.

Later, you'll put some of these resources to work as you bring your brand to market. But let's not get ahead of ourselves.

For a start, you just need to keep building a list of anyone and everyone you and your family know who has a job in the area that interests you – or who lives in the area that interests you. Lives in the area? Really.

When Bruce started job-hunting, he was a summer guest with Bob's family in New Jersey. Bruce went into New York City every day and had informational interviews.

Every night, he had a great time in New Jersey – with Bob and his friends. We call that a win/win.

He learned what the job market was like a year before he had to find one. He also learned that maybe he didn't want to work in New York City.

Then, over Christmas break, it was Regan's turn to have Bruce as a guest. Regan's dad was a Chicago ad executive – and he provided terrific connections. Bruce had to make the call – but now he knew who to call.

Those two resources – college friends – were critical to getting a jump on the job market. That spring, Bruce received job offers from the three biggest agencies in Chicago.

Be Resourceful in Getting Your Resources.

What is it you think you want to do?

Where do you think you might want to do it?

You might want to talk to your parents, some of their very good friends – people you know well – and maybe a favorite aunt or uncle – see who they might know.

The earlier you start, the better you'll do. Still figuring it out? OK, even that's a good start for a conversation with someone who is already doing well in business. Got advice?

When there's lead time, it's OK to ask. Early on, Bruce could simply say, *"I want to know what I need to know so that you might be interested in hiring me next year."*

Not next week. Not next month. Next year.

Knowledge is one of your most valuable resources.

Recently, some friends had a just-about-to graduate daughter learning video editing. We put her in touch with a friend who was a working video editor. What did she need to know to be a valuable editing assistant? Video formats!

As it turned out, at that moment the industry was wrestling with video materials showing up in a wide range of formats – an assistant had to be able to help deal with all the technical aspects of collation, conversion, and keeping track.

What's the point of this knowledge? Try this. Nobody was teaching that stuff!! They were busy with editing techniques and the history of film and all kinds of this and that.

Students were shooting and editing their little senior videos and documentaries. Well and good.

But somebody who showed up with an understanding and familiarity with those current technical issues – which was what they needed beginning video editors for – that person was going to the front of the hiring line! Golly, don't you want to see my senior video project? Not particularly.

Sometimes, the right resources can provide you with the kind of in-the-moment marketplace knowledge that is critical to knowing what the market is looking for.

What are your resources? You won't know until you start looking for them.

But you can start with the name, address, phone number, name of the company, job title, and email address of the people you need to know. Database. Database. Database.

Be resourceful.

Things To Do:

• *Review Your Notes. You were taking notes, right? If not, do that. Now. Then you can review them.*

What are your Talents?

What are your Interests?

What are your Goals?

What is your Experience?

What are your Resources? Go get 'em TIGER!

• **Database. Database. Database.** Keep building it, and talk about it with your friends. You don't know what you don't know. Make it a part of your conversation; you might be surprised who your friends (and their parents) know.

• **Read all about it.** We've mentioned a few books and opened up a few new topics. Why not pick up a book that interests you? Or Google a magazine article on a topic that's related to your general career objective?

• **Start thinking about *Brand You!*** Look at those notes again. Where do you think you fit in the marketplace?

Hey, that's the next chapter!

20: Understanding The Modern Marketplace.

MOORE'S LAW ISN'T JUST CHANGING COMPUTERS. It's changing everything!

When your parents went job hunting 20-some years ago, the economy was different. The media was different. The jobs were different. The marketplace was different.

Welcome to the 21st Century.

Creative Destruction. A State of Constant Rebirth.

The Phoenix is much like today's marketplace.

New business models, new software, new technology, and all of the above. Need to catch a cab? Wait a minute, I'll get Uber. Or Lyft. Rideshare is changing an industry that has been here for over one hundred years.

In this case, computers, GPS, and payments via mobile phone combined to create a new way of doing an old business.

You need to start getting in touch with that marketplace – which shouldn't be too hard, because you're living in it.

But pay attention! You need to get a feel for the changes going on as you look for those that work to your advantage. Here are two examples.

The Vergara Vision.

When you start to study a market, you need knowledge. When Marcelo Vergara graduated from the University of Kansas, he looked before he made the leap.

He spent time developing an accurate view of the market where he was going job hunting. He looked before he leaped.

His initial target career area was desktop publishing – with a smooth possible move into digital design and marketing.

Here's his advice. *"Pick your target employers. Be selective. Choose quality firms. Research them thoroughly. Learn about their top managers. Check the trade press (online and off). Check local business papers. Ask for their newsletter. Learn all you can about your top choices."*

Based on that knowledge, he said you need to *"Develop a strategic marketing plan for your own campaign. Your objective is to get an interview."*

Mark created a Web site/print campaign. But instead of putting a normal résumé online, he designed a real site. He became his own *Brand You!* Here's what he had to say:

"Make yourself the product or service. Brand your skills. Brand your personality."

Then, Mark worked to get his target involved. *"Try to get your target to interact with you before you even meet.*

"Figure out a way to get them to send you an e-mail instead of the other way around. This business is all about relationships.

"When you get an interview, tell them how you did it and show them your strategy. It shows you have discipline, maturity, and understanding. Those are good things."

Note how important it is to target. Marcelo had a strategic focus and plan for his "brand."

He matched his brand up with the marketplace and emphasized important values like "interactivity."

Also notice that he set achievable goals – get an interview, build relationships. With upfront research, he knew who and where his target was. His planning had a target customer focus.

Marcelo knew what he wanted, and he knew that there was a solid and growing segment of the marketplace with desktop publishing and web design.

Our next example, wasn't quite so sure.

Where's the Growth?

If you look at a big aggregate number like GNP or ad spending, those big numbers show slow movement. There's growth, but it's kind of slow and steady.

However, if you "lift the hood" and look under those big aggregate numbers, you often see a lot of activity.

Tracey Aurich, a Penn State grad, found her first advertising job by looking at specialty markets. She found one that was a good fit and growing strong... pharmaceutical advertising.

In 2014, direct-to-consumer ad spending hit $4.53 billion – up about 18% from $3.83 billion in 2013. They're hiring.

In fact, one drug maker ranked among the top Ten advertisers, ahead of Verizon, Toyota, and Chrysler – just a hair behind L'Oreal – with a 23% leap in 2014 spending. Who? Pfizer!

Tracey observed that within the overall markets, you want to find the growth sectors, *"and within these markets, you can find a career... It's just a matter of knowing if an opportunity exists.*

"Case in point... I fell into my first account services position at a pharmaceutical advertising agency – a specialty I didn't even know existed."

It hadn't been big and growing until fairly recently.

Tracey mentions a bit of history. Previously *"pharmaceutical advertising involved promoting prescription and over-the-counter medications to healthcare professionals only. But... legal changes... made the field even more interesting. Now that direct-to-consumer advertising is permitted, this specialty is becoming better known."*

Note How Fast Things Change.

Tracey entered a field that didn't do consumer advertising a decade or so earlier. Now she's involved in it in a big way – participating in a revolution in pharmaceutical marketing.

How do you find those opportunities? If you have a crystal ball, turn it on, and skip this next section.

Otherwise, here are four things to look at:

1. **Advertising-to-Sales Ratios.** Most other marketing spending is harder to measure, so take a look at the advertising-to-sales (A-to-S) ratio of various companies – even if you're not going into advertising. It's a good measure of where some of your best opportunities might be.

   You can find A-to-S ratios on the internet and in trade magazines like *Advertising Age*. Their "Leading Advertisers" issues contain a lot of useful information. You can get the latest *Ad Age FactPack* PDF at www.adage.com.

2. **Search out High-Growth Industries and Businesses.** Look for areas where things are happening. Right now, the financial industry, wine industry, travel industry, and pharmaceutical industries are experiencing huge expansion – but not everywhere. Healthcare? It's up and down.

   Remember Mark looking into desktop publishing? Sometimes it's only certain companies within an industry. You'll want to know which. And where.

   To learn more about high-growth industries, you might want to check thestreet.com – a powerful place to get ideas about high-growth businesses. The site was rated number one by the *New York Times* and gives wide-ranging opinions about the world's business opportunities and stock market projections.

   You can log on for a one-month free trial subscription. Another valuable resource is motleyfool.com, with an idea-a-minute, plus droll humor and sharp analysis of emerging markets. And speaking of...

3. Emerging Markets.

When companies are literally inventing themselves, it's sometimes impossible to get someone with experience.

So, as they say in football drafts, you go for "the best available athlete." If you're smart, aggressive, flexible, and resourceful enough to track these companies down (they're too busy to look for you), you just might be who they're looking for – if they had the time to look.

Other Things You Can Do.

Want to know more? Try these basic approaches.

Read All about It.

Read trade and business magazines. "Marketplace," the second section of the *Wall Street Journal* (WSJ), is usually a good place to turn to when you see a copy.

Get familiar with some of the cutting-edge business magazines like *Wired* and *Fast Company*, as well as the standbys *Business Week* and *Fortune*. If you're going into business, why not start reading what business people read?

At first, only bits and pieces will make sense to you. Then the connections will start to kick in.

Your brain is changing, remember?

Get your antennae tuned – try to think about what's coming and who might be hiring.

Study the Top Companies in Your Town, City, or Region.

You may be surprised by how much opportunity is right where you live – or nearby. Many of these companies are privately held, or you don't hear about the larger company that owns the brands you're familiar with.

Discover the leading companies in your area – as well as the hot new players.

See what you find. You might be surprised.

The simple fact in a complicated world is that the more you learn about your market, the better you'll understand it and the opportunities that market offers.

Understanding the Job Market.

The marketplace isn't just industries, it's the jobs within those industries. By now, because of how fast things change, you know that any list we print will probably be a bit out-of-date as soon as we print it.

However… we're going to offer a few generic observations about job areas that have traditionally gone under-leveraged:

- **Field Marketing.** "On-the-ground" marketing is still needed by many companies, such as franchise organizations and beverage marketers. People move up. Openings happen. Often.

- **Marketing Services.** New types of ad agencies are evolving – only we don't call them that. The *Mad Men* days might be over, but there's still a lot going on: Events and Experiential, Internet agencies, branding firms, and unique creative boutiques. Hey, how about "Shopper Marketing?" There's a new one.

- **Media Companies.** Thank you, Marshall McLuhan. As traditional media works to shift to digital, and new channels and content sources emerge, opportunities are opening up almost everywhere. And they *always* need someone to help sell. Selling media is a tough job, but they're hiring. They also tend to use lots of interns.

- **And So On.** As we were writing this, "Big Data" was getting big. Companies still want sales promotion agencies, public relations firms, database marketing, direct marketing, and, of course, website developers.

The more you learn, the more clues you'll get – and you really will start to understand your market.

Find out what's happening. And with whom.

Narrowing Your Target Market.

Strategy is about choice. As you acquire more information, you can start making a few choices.

By now, you have an initial understanding of the complexity of the marketplace – and the speed of change. Yet, with a bit of focus, you can extract a few firms and a few names and start to move forward.

The Top Firms – you need to identify the biggest and best firms in the career area that interests you. Though you might not end up there, they're best equipped to give you relatively good information on "what we're looking for." They'll make you smarter. And speaking of relatives…

Friends & Family – do we know anybody yet? Just one or two names for a start will be wonderful. Again, these are people who can "make you smarter."

Remember, you're still learning about the marketplace.

You're going to start developing some thoughts on where you can make the best connection. Ask around.

A few other things are happening.

- **You're getting smarter.** You're beginning to understand the marketplace. Sure, it's big and chaotic, but if we can focus a bit, some things will start to line up. It's just like "how to eat an elephant." How's that? One bite at a time.

- **You're starting to understand.** You see the dynamics and how you might match up. Your "T.I.G.E.R." exercise helped you to start thinking about what you might offer a company. You're starting to see connections.

- As you focus on a narrower market, with a few more specifics, you're slowly beginning to understand what they might be looking for in the entry-level job market.

Now let's add two other things to our target database:

Geography & Opportunity.

Here are the next two things we need to know:

1. **Geography**

2. **Opportunity**

Is there a particular part of the country where you want to work – or need to work?

Is there a unique set of circumstances that creates an opportunity that you can leverage?

Let's give ourselves a quick Geography lesson.

Do any of the following apply?
❏ Your hometown.
❏ Your college town – if it's not your hometown.
❏ Locations of the leading firms in your target industry.

For some, this will be helpful. If you're looking for a sports marketing job in your hometown, your target has just been better defined. You know where to look. You might not find it, but you know where to look. This is progress.

Next, you need to look for opportunities. What does this mean? It means — do we have any match-ups out there?

For example, alumni of your school.

This is a genuine opportunity. They'll talk to you. They'll help. In general, you can immediately establish a common ground with this target. So you need to do one more thing:

❏ Identify a number of your school's graduates now working in the field that you're currently interested in.

As we said, they're likely to help you – even if it's only to give you some good advice – or a new name to contact.

If you're going to school in a big city, your job might be right where you're going to school. Or maybe not.

Without knowing a single thing about you, we know there will be companies or places where you have better opportunities than others. Watch for them. That's opportunity in action.

As you research prospective target markets, you're going to be learning. And the more you learn about possible targets, the more opportunities will surface.

For example, if there's a place to live while you look for a job, (a relative has a guest room and is okay with a visit of a week or two) that place will have better opportunity.

The Match Game.

See what's going on? By digging into your potential target markets, and learning every step of the way, things are falling into place.

Now, to state the obvious, the sooner you start on this, the better. This is a game best begun early in your junior year. Not late in your senior year. Or after graduation.

But whenever it is, you now have to start working your network and look for matches in the marketplace.

You're looking to create a better match between what you offer and what the marketplace needs.

And now, just as you start to focus… go wide.

As You Focus, Expand Your Job Horizon.

This isn't contradictory. As you focus on what you want to do, you also need to expand your horizons.

Looking for sports marketing with a minor league baseball team? What's wrong with hockey? Or the NBA D-League?

You need to expand and narrow your target simultaneously.

For example, let's assume you want a writing job. You like to write and think you're good at it.

Once upon a time, the most obvious writing job was as an ad copywriter – but don't stop there. Look at other opportunities.

Companies need newsletters. Hospitals need health bulletins. Marketers need support materials.

John's daughter was a writer moving to Portland, OR. John had a friend who knew Dan Wieden of Nike's agency, Wieden + Kennedy. As a courtesy, Dan got her an interview at Nike and guess what? She got a job there! As a tech writer.

Just do it. When you look under the hood, there are a lot more real opportunities than you realize.

Now, what if writing is just one of the things you do?

Joy went to Temple in Philadelphia. She's now a PR account exec in New York City. Here's her story:

"My plan was to be an ad copywriter – but toward my senior year in college I had the nagging suspicion that, as much as I enjoyed writing, if I had to do it all day, every day, it would drive me bonkers.

"So when I finished school, I decided to freelance while conducting my job search. It allowed me to sample different jobs, and that's how I ended up in a small but visible PR firm.

"In PR I could be on both the creative side and the business side. I could develop strategy. I could plan campaigns. I could write, and I could be the client contact.

"This diversity is why I chose PR."

Joy also discovered that sometimes there can be bigger opportunities in smaller places.

She added, *"In a small firm I could learn a lot quickly, gaining responsibility by grabbing it.*

"Even if your aspirations are to work in a large agency – which mine always were – consider the benefits of starting small."

There can be more opportunities than you realize in today's modern marketplace. All you have to do is narrow your focus – and expand your horizons.

Try to hold that thought – without your head exploding.

Things To Do:

* **Database. Database. Database.** Keep building it. Try to add more categories of connections: Alumni. Companies in Emerging Markets. Companies in your geographic target market. Friends of friends. Leading firms in your target category (if you don't know anyone, start with the HR people and their Web site). Random opportunities. Wider horizons. (That was kind of alphabetical.)

* **Read all about it.** Look for more sources on your target category. Find relevant articles and trade journals. Ask your instructor what you should be reading.

* **Keep thinking about *Brand You!*** You probably don't know yet, but are you starting to feel where you might fit? Good. Naturally, you don't really know until you get that first offer, but when it comes to being judged as a candidate for that job, maybe you need to be just a bit better.

Good thing that's the next section!

21. Increase Your Market Value.

IT'S NOT ALL GRADE POINT. Getting good grades is part of it – but it's but more for what you're learning, not some number on a four-year scorecard. (Grad school, that's different.)

What a company hiring you wants to know is simply this – are you the best person for the job that needs doing?

They don't just want you "book smart," they want you real world smart. So, between now and then, how do you improve your chances? Here's what we'll focus on in this chapter.

- Making the Most of Your Degree

- Internships and Summer Jobs

- Networking

- Extras

Let's look at them one by one.

Making the Most of Your Degree.

When you're a freshman, things seem pretty much laid out for you. They are. You're told to take certain courses. And you do.

But what your advisor might not tell you – and maybe you're not ready to think about it – is that you should be mapping out future courses according to your career interest.

That sounds fine, but do you really know what that career interest is or even will be? You're starting to think about it.

Much like anything else, there's a learning curve regarding your courses and career interest.

Usually, that learning curve begins your freshman year.

Some are lucky enough to know from the start – and they're steady on that path. Good for them

The rest of us, we kind of have to figure it out as we go – and we have to get ready at the same time we're still figuring it out.

There are several ways you can increase your market value – even if you're still figuring it out. For now, let's assume you're aiming at the right general area.

It's like you kind of know the neighborhood – but you just don't have the exact address yet. So, chances are, you have about two years to prepare for your place in the marketplace – two years to find the right match between your "brand" and what's out there.

That's two years to do a bit of "brand-building," starting with that degree you're working hard to get.

Here's what you need to do.

1. Take the right courses

2. Get the right minor with your major

3. Get involved and volunteer

4. Look into national student competitions

5. Comb your campus

Let's get started.

1. Take the Right Courses.

• As a Freshman, you start with prescribed and required courses because you must. During this first year you begin to learn what you like, and – just as important – what you don't like.

• Sophomore year, your interests are usually coming more into focus. You're still taking required courses, but now is the time to consider – or take – specific courses in your interest area – usually an intro course.

• Junior year, you should be making headway in your major field of study. (Reading this book, we're going to assume you're somewhere in your sophomore or junior year. If you're a senior, read faster. If you've graduated, read real fast!!)

• If it's your Senior year, we hope you're settled well into your major and career interest. That's the way it's supposed to work. But… people change. And so do majors.

So, first question. Are you getting all the coursework that your school says your major requires?

Second question. Is your major a match with what you want to be doing? If so, you can check off this box. √

If not, well, the start of solving a problem is knowing what problem to solve. Sometimes, the majors offered aren't a match for what you want to do.

Bruce had that problem. Back in the day, there really wasn't much of an ad program at his university – so he majored in psychology and took other courses to fill in.

He ended up with two ad courses, a screenwriting course, and a marketing course offered in the Business school. He also figured that since advertising was about understanding who you were talking to, a major in psychology would be helpful. It was.

He built his major. You might have to do the same.

Today, for example, it may be that some of the new digital technology and "Big Data" activity isn't in the catalog yet – or maybe it's in another department.

You may have to find a way to make it happen. Maybe a summer course. Or some of the new online resources.

The point is, you want to make your major match your career objective.

Do we agree? Let's keep moving.

2. Get the Right Minor with Your Major.

This may be part of the answer. Today's widening variety of opportunity, means you may want something a bit outside your major. Try to identify the courses that apply and see what's involved in taking them.

Sometimes it's easy. And sometimes you run into a thicket of bureaucracy and objections. Sorry, you're not in that department – only room for those majoring, etc.

For this one, check carefully with your advisor and, perhaps, an advisor in the department of your minor. Here are some thoughts as to the kind of minors that can help:

- If you're interested in account management, psychology, sociology, or marketing may offer valuable minors.

- For creative work, English (creative writing), art, film, computer graphics, and psychology may be suitable.

- For media or research, try economics, statistics, marketing, psychology, or sociology. Those might be a good fit.

- For all of us, this is a business where presentation is key.

- You might want to take a speech class. Or two.

- But there's even more you can do. Because there's more to school than taking classes.

  We bet you know that already.

3. Get Involved. Volunteer.

One way you increase your value is by getting involved. Join clubs and organizations, particularly those in your field.

And, once you get in the habit of volunteering your time, you might find you like it. And don't think you have to stop once you've started work.

A True Story - From Alderman to Oval Office.

At the start of his career, right after graduating, Bruce volunteered to write brochures for a local Chicago candidate for alderman – he won.

That led to other freelance work in politics – most of it done for free. Eight years later, it led to a paying job as Creative Director for a President of the United States. You never know.

4. Look into Student Competitions.

Now, there are more and more student contests. You get to work hard on a "real world" problem, and measure your efforts against other students nationwide – sometimes internationally.

This can be very valuable experience. You work on a deadline with a professionally-prepared project description.

One example that we think is extremely valuable is the AAF/NSAC – the American Ad Federation National Student Advertising Competition (AAF/NSAC), or, "The College World Series of Advertising."

Even though its emphasis is advertising, anyone in PR, MarCom, or StratCom in general, should look into it.

- The client is a big national – or international – company.

- The briefing material will be first-rate. It will be a real marketing problem – the kind people pay real money to solve. It's not another silly hot sauce ad.

- The competition is tough. In any given year, well over 100 schools may compete. There's participation by most of the ad programs at US colleges and universities – big and small.

- The work load is "real world." Schools form agency-like communications teams. Many think it's the best real-world advertising experience offered at universities.

- We agree – and we recommend it highly. Though we also guarantee that some nights – when you're up very late working on a plans book that's due in a week, you'll wonder if you should have listened to us.

- We also recommend you go to the Regional Competition and see what the other teams did. Even if you aren't on "the traveling team," go sit and watch. And learn.

Today, there is a growing number of other "real world" competitions. We recommend you find out about as many as you can – and enter the ones that seem to offer the best learning experience for your chosen career path.

Then, you'll see how you measure up. Doing well in these contests is a sure-fire way to increase your market value.

5. Comb Your Campus.

Beyond participating in competitions, you need to search out, work for, or volunteer your time to key campus organizations and groups. Here are some examples:

• **Campus media.** There's more all the time. It may include your campus newspaper, radio station, television station, or even an allied department on campus that works with the media– like sports information. They may need your help.

• **Work-study programs.** These often allow you to work within your major or minor department while going to school.

• **Internships.** More on this in a bit. Remember, it may be possible to take more than one internship over the course of two or three years.

• **Other campus organizations.** These can help differentiate you as a brand, while simultaneously improving your skills. See what your school has to offer.

• **Join a student agency.** Or start one.

Ever hear of GSD&M in Austin? They started as ad students at the University of Texas who liked working together. They started in a tiny office in an out-of-the-way office park. Now you're looking at their building – Idea City.

Today, more and more schools have some kind of student agency. Think about joining. Learn. Make some noise. Have fun. Create great samples. Start working on a great portfolio.

And while you're doing it, you'll be increasing your value.

Internships & Summer Jobs.

Here are two good ways to get the kind of practical experience that will further increase your value:

1. **Internships**

2. **Summer Jobs**

   During your college career, try to get more than one of each.

1. **Internships.** Internships often provide valuable work experience and contacts. They also help to provide additional definition to the "commodity" that's a university degree. Try to get at least two before you graduate.

   If you're applying for a job at a TV station and they see that you interned at a TV station, that fact jumps off your résumé and moves you toward the head of the line.

   And your internship can keep going.

It's not uncommon for student interns to continue working for the sponsoring company after the internship is over. It's a "try before you buy" that often works out well for everybody.

Differentiating a "Commodity."

As we've said, your degree is, in many ways, a commodity. As a practical matter, it's virtually identical to all the other degrees from your classmates at your school and other schools.

Activities that differentiate you from those classmates are often considered the most valuable by those making decisions about who gets the jobs.

For example, production companies look for someone who has done apprentice or intern work in the production field.

Larger media companies, such as major local TV stations, often look for people who have trained at smaller media companies, such as local cable TV stations and radio stations.

Make note of these special experiences. You should also consider adding those you plan on developing in the near future. This will help keep you on track in your career pursuit.

Create Your Own Internships.

The importance of digging up internships, sometimes literally creating them, is dramatized by Gregg Friedmann, a Penn State grad – now a pharmaceutical copywriter. Here's his story.

"Odds are that somewhere near you, there is an ad agency or marketing department willing to give you an internship.

"During my junior year I called a wide selection of ad agencies close to where I live and asked about internships. One local agency gave me a shot, even though they'd never had an intern before.

"Thanks to the contacts I made during that summer internship, I not only got a lead on my first job, but I am now work-

ing at the same agency I had interned at years before."

Here's some advice from Gregg on how to make it happen:

"When you call the agency, you'll get the receptionist. Ask to speak to the person in charge of internships. If there is no such person, ask to speak to the creative director or the account planner or someone in the field you're suited for.

"Don't let go of this contact, even if they don't return your call. Send an email, a letter, or tell your story on voicemail. If it seems fruitless after awhile, move on to the next person and agency.

"Beyond arranging for an internship yourself, go to your school's career placement office, or your department's internship office or director. Make your plans known, and make repeated visits to obtain the latest information on available internships."

Whether you secure an internship from your school, or by working the phones on your own, the main point is to get at least one during your college career. Two is even better.

2. **Summer Jobs.** Don't get just any summer job. Try to get one in in the career area you want to be working in. Even if you're sweeping up, answering the phone, making copies, making coffee, and sitting in meetings only occasionally, that experience isn't just money in the bank, it's solid gold on the resumé. Even if they didn't pay you. Or barely paid you.
   This is where your real first job may be.

And here is where you may be able to expand your own experiences, adding more substance to "Brand You!"

By the way, the time to start looking for a summer job is during your Winter Break. Or sooner.

3. **And Summer Trips.** If you need to work most of the summer to help with school costs, consider what you can do in a week or two.
   One week of informational interviewing and visiting the city where you think you want to work can teach you a lot.

Networking.

On some levels, it's as simple as the law of averages.

The way to get connected is to get connected. Build your knowledge. Build your connections. Build your relationships.

The more people you know, the better your odds. You'll have more to choose from, and be able to make better judgments.

"It's who you know" is truer than you may think. In a nutshell, networking is meeting new people in a professional context, forging a connection, building those relationships over time, and providing value to each other.

This skill is essential because, long term, a surprising percentage of each person's success is due to "human engineering"– your personality, communication ability, negotiation skills, and emotional intelligence.

Technical knowledge? Some say a mere 15%. Frankly, we hope it's a bit more than that.

The Strength of Weak Ties.

In his classic 1974 book, *Getting a Job,* Mark Granovetter had some fascinating insights based on a survey.

• 56% of the people who got jobs got them through some sort of personal connection;

• 20% got them through a formal hiring process;

• 20% applied directly.

Now it gets interesting.

Connections = Better Jobs.

Personal connections tended to result in better jobs at better salaries. But those connections were not necessarily strong or close. They tended to be weaker, "friend of a friend" type connections.

But even though they weren't close or strong, they were close enough and strong enough to open the doors – and that was the key.

So don't be bothered if some of the connections you connect with are a bit distant – that's normal.

People Like to Connect.

One more thing. While it is a bit of an imposition, most professionals enjoy making the connections that result in someone getting their start. It's a source of satisfaction.

Years from now, when you're asked to help the son or daughter of "a friend of a friend," you may get the same satisfaction.

Some Networking Guidelines.

Here are some useful networking guidelines:

1. **Find a Mentor.**

2. **Get to Know Important Others.**

3. **Look for People from Whom You Can Learn.**

Let's take them one at a time.

1. **Find a Mentor.** As we've mentioned repeatedly (Database. Database. Database.), it's vital that you begin developing your contacts and references – your network.
   Some will come from personal networking, which means you should be active in appropriate local marketing organizations, including those in your college and region.
   Others might come from those you have contact with daily

– your professors. You should also remember that finding contacts, mentors, or a network of colleagues won't work if you wait until you're a senior.

You need to begin developing those relationships early on.

2. **Get to Know "Important Others."** Start by targeting key people, such as your profs or guest speakers, or those you are able meet at professional meetings in your local area. Write them. Use your 3-Ups. Keep up with them and what they're doing. Maintain their contact. Don't lose touch. Got email? Use it.

Terryl Ross, a Syracuse University graduate, has this to say about the importance of networking:

"Establishing a network with people in your field is the key to starting and maintaining a successful career.

"Of the jobs and contracts I have had in my eight years in recreation, 85% have come from the networks I created.

"Establish networks by joining clubs, attending conferences, meeting alumni, and volunteering for projects related to advertising.

"Keep in touch with people you meet. Send emails, cards, and examples of what you have produced. Ask for advice.

"Establish networks in other fields where you have an interest. Remember, it's never too early to start building your network, and your network can never be too large."

3. **Look for People from Whom You Can Learn.** During your first few jobs, it's critical to find people you can learn from. At the beginning of your career, learning is even more important than earning.

These days, it's not as easy as it used to be. Why? Because everybody's busier, so it's harder to find that time when you can really hear what more experienced people can teach you.

But it's one of the most important things you can do.

We'll finish this by repeating a powerful quote:

"People who have diverse networks tend to be promoted faster and get new jobs more quickly."

That's from the CEO of a "behavioral analytics" company. Seems like something worth remembering.

Extras.

It doesn't stop there. Here are a few more ways you might consider adding to your value – though some might cost a bit.

1. Interview Extras
2. Developing Your Portfolio
3. An Advanced Degree

Remember, you're competing against a lot of other smart, dedicated people. And your target market is always looking for people who have something extra. Give them what they want.

1. **Interview Extras.** When you go on an interview, you want to be able to show something more than your diploma, GPA, and a résumé. Here are some thoughts on giving your presentation something extra.

- **Produced Work.** Through your classes and experiences, what work have you actually produced that warrants notice?

    Are there posters or support materials for some project you worked on? They can help dramatize the event.

    Did you put together a marketing plan for a campus group that helped stimulate the group's constructive thinking about its future? Did you spearhead the fraternity recruitment drive?

    Have you helped someone solve a marketing or advertising problem? Be ready to show or discuss these achievements.

    Consider one-page case histories for those projects.

    Look for ways to visualize and dramatize accomplishments. No accomplishments to visualize and dramatize? Looks like you've got one more goal.

- **Letters and Commendations.**
As you work or volunteer throughout your college career, you'll develop references, those who can and will speak kindly of you as a coworker and person. For good reason. Often they're pleased to write a letters about it.

If you've been particularly successful on a certain project, try to get a letter of commendation to add to the letters of recommendation. Oh, and a photo or two might be nice, too.

2. **Developing Your Portfolio.** We'll cover this in more depth in the next section, but you need to start working on this.

Portfolios have been standard for those interested in the creative side of advertising for decades, but now, almost every meaningful job in the communications field is looking for some sort of portfolio.

Here's how Gregg Friedmann describes it:

"Your book is a binder or portfolio case filled with samples of your work. It's the one thing that will make or break you more than anything else. So make the most of it.

"You should start thinking about it as early in your college career as possible."

Chris Smith, adds: *"When should you start working on your book? Start yesterday. You can stop the same day you accept the Rolex at your retirement party. Never stop.*

"Show your work to as many industry people as possible, and then heed their advice."

The advanced advertising portfolio schools have that as their main objective - helping you develop a "book" good enough to land a job. Only now, almost everyone needs a "book."

What if you're not a "Creative?" These days, that doesn't matter, they still want to see examples of your work.

And, if you think about it, almost every job in MarCom and StratCom is – to some extent – "creative."

Today, everyone needs a portfolio. And it has to be good. Once, an AAF/NSAC plans book would impress a recruiter.

Now, it needs to be even better – additionally edited, and sometimes more. For example, now you need a summary – verbal or written. AAF Plans Books can be a bit daunting to interviewers who aren't familiar with them.

3. **Think About an Advanced Degree (Maybe).** An advanced degree isn't for everyone, nor does it guarantee career success. But for some people, it helps.

   Advanced degrees like MBAs, MAs, and MFAs can provide you with additional skills, prospects, and a certain degree of prestige – depending on who you're talking to.

   Going into marketing? Consider an MBA.

   For ad agency work, an MBA for account execs or a portfolio school for creatives may be a good decision.

   There are now a number of schools, like Miami Ad School, or VCU BrandCenter, that do inter-disciplinary work and teach account planning.

   Some specialties look for advanced degrees.

   For example, many market research companies will prefer advanced degrees, and most marketing companies look for MBAs in marketing.

Good News! Your Company Might Help with Your MBA!

Let's say, you've just finished paying tuition for your under-grad degree, and you want to get started on your career.

So two more years of school may not be quite what you had in mind. Don't worry, a lot of people feel that way.

In fact, quite a few get their MBAs while already working. Most cities have MBA programs designed for people who are working 9 to 5.

They feature lighter course loads and evening classes. Many companies have programs where they'll pitch in and help with the tuition.

You might even let people know you're interested in getting an MBA during your interview.

Studying Up. Following Up. Keeping It Up.

There's a lot to do here, increasing your value step by step. In fact, once you graduate and get that first job, your brand-building doesn't stop. Because that first job is just the first step toward where you're headed. You have to keep increasing your market value.

Cody's Career Path.

Here's a typical example. Cody Aufricht's first job was with a small agency in Midland, Texas — it was a small business-to-business ad agency specializing in oil and gas and financial advertising.

Cody spent his first two years as an account exec, moving up to Senior AE and then to VP/Partner two years later.

Three years after that, he was Ad Manager of International Telecharge, Inc., a $300 million telecom company. Two years after that, he was their Manager of Marketing Services.

From there, Cody moved to PHH Vehicle Management Services, Inc.; then, he became Director of Marketing of Today's Temporary, Inc. a $180 million staffing company.

Now, he develops and directs overall marketing strategy for their 120 offices. He directs all market research programs and manages all marketing communications.

Cody had a fairly common career path:

• He started small where he could learn the business.

• He proved himself enough to move up (to manager).
• He moved up again, this time to director.
Step by step, he increased the value of his brand.
It's a process that starts in college – but it doesn't stop.

Things To Do:

Let's review the various ways we can add value.

❏ **Take the right courses.** What's on your list for next semester?

❏ **The right minor with your major.** Ditto.

❏ **Volunteering.** Write down a few extra things you could do. Think about it. Do one of them.

❏ **Student Competitions.** Is there an AAF/NSAC team? Are you on it? Go to one of their meetings – or talk to the Faculty Advisor – or one of the team members. Find out what other competitions are out there. Learn about them.

❏ **Other Campus Activities.** What else could you be doing? Don't do all of it. Pick one. Think about it.

❏ **Internships.** What would be your ideal internship? What kind of company? Can you create an internship?

❏ **Summer Job.** What? Where? If you are going to be otherwise employed, where would you like to go for some "informational interviews?" How can you make that happen?

❏ **Networking – Find a Mentor.** Think about it. Is there an instructor on campus who can get you started?

❏ **Networking – Important Others.** Who? Give it some thought. Database. Database. Database.

❏ **Networking – People You Can Learn From.** Ditto.

22. Take Your Brand To Market.

LET'S START WITH A STRATEGY.

Strategy is, essentially, informed choice. So maybe it's time to start making a few Brand You! decisions.

Maybe you've done a bit of strategy development as part of your coursework, maybe not, but I'd like to start with a favorite quote – from *The Mind of the Strategist* by Kenichi Ohmae. He was the former head of McKinsey in Japan. Very smart.

"In business as on the battlefield, the object of strategy is to bring about the conditions most favorable to one's own side.

"In strategic thinking, one first seeks a clear understanding of the particular character of each element of a situation, and then makes the fullest possible use of human brainpower to <u>restructure the elements in the most advantageous way.</u>

"Phenomena and events in the real world do not always fit a linear model. Hence, the most reliable means of dissecting a situation into its constituent parts, and then reassembling them in the desired pattern is not a step-by-step methodology such as systems analysis.

*"Rather, it is **that ultimate non-linear thinking tool, the human brain.***

*"No matter how difficult or unprecedented the problem, a breakthrough to the best possible solution can come only from a combination of **rational analysis** based on the real nature of things, and **imaginative re-integration of all the different items into a new pattern using non-linear brainpower.***"

It's a pretty heavy quote – there's quite a lot in it.

For a start, let's focus on two things:

One: *the goal of strategy is to bring about the conditions most favorable to one's own side.*

Two: *rational analysis based on the real nature of things,*

We'll get to imaginative re-integration and non-linear brainpower later. Let's think about our objective – our goal.

We want to *bring about the conditions most favorable to one's own side.* Right?

And we're going to be real about it. OK?

All right, time for some fun.

Your Brand You! Target.

First, it would be kind of nice if we had a clue about where we're going. That work for you?

OK then, let's look at the target industries where you think you'd like to work.

Complete this sentence:

In a perfect world, I'd like to work in (Target Industry)

_____.

Got it? We may not get there, but you've got a BHAG.

You've got the address, let's get the nearby neighborhood. Other industries that might be interesting are:

Alternate Target Industry #1_____,

Alternate Target Industry #2 _____,

and Alternate Target Industry #3 _____.

Geographically, given your home address, resources, connections, and so on… where, at present, is the most reasonable place for this to happen?

"Best Bet" Market _____.

Where are other places where this could happen?

Alternate Market #1 _____,

Alternate Market #2 _____,

and Alternate Market #3 _____.

150

Hey, it looks to me like you've got the beginnings of a Brand You Target Statement.

My Brand You! Objective is to get a starting job in (Target Industry) _____,
    and I will also take a look at:
Alternate Target Industry #1_____,
Alternate Target Industry #2 _____,
and Alternate Target Industry #3 _____.
    At present, the best place for me to look is
"Best Bet" Market _____
    But I'll also keep in mind opportunities in
Alternate Market #1 _____,
Alternate Market #2 _____,
and Alternate Market #3 _____.

You can change your mind, or make any modification you want, but you now have a target to aim at.

Your Brand You! Personality.

OK, who is Brand You? You've done some logo exercises, and you just spent a bit of time on that T.I.G.E.R. form.

Let's ask a few questions – and you can keep reading this chapter if you want, but it's time to write down some thoughts. And realize that when I say, "Pick a Word," you can really pick as many words as you want.

But you may be surprised that some of the first stuff that comes to mind – in this case – will be close to what you want. So here goes...

    Pick a Word
    Pick another Word
    Pick a Phrase
    Pick a Goal or Dream (your BHAG)

Say something funny (or insulting) about yourself.

Write 'em down – and we'll let it settle for a bit.

In case you wondered, here's what I'd write down:

Pick a Word - *Jazz*

Pick another Word - *Hip*

Pick a Phrase – *Life is a Team Sport.*

Pick a Goal or Dream – *Change lives with "Brand You!"*

Say something funny (or insulting) about yourself.

Can't Sing. Don't Care. (That's the title of my CD.)

OK, your turn.

While you're thinking, let's wrestle with your next strategic challenge – *differentiation.*

Brand You! Challenge #1: Differentiation.

It's that commodity problem again. How do we take who you are and make it Brand You! – unique and memorable?

Let's start with a story. Why?

Because *stories teach.* We can say stuff, and use all sorts of adjectives and slogans. But if we tell a story, that kind of gets remembered.

Remember when I told you a story about going to my first accounting class and realizing that I needed to figure out what else I was going to do? Because that wasn't it.

Yes, you remember. Stories are easy to remember.

So... what's your story?

Your Brand Story.

Your Brand Story is an interesting way of presenting you, your brand and your brand personality. Your story will give a focus to "Brand You!" In a few comfortable sentences, it lets you introduce yourself and position yourself in a memorable way.

Every brand needs a story – including you.

It's a way to introduce yourself to people who might want to hire you. Or meet you. Or remember you.

Why is this important? Bill Dauphanis of the firm Pricewaterhouse/Coopers LLP has some insights, *"Brands are built around stories. And stories of identity – who we are, where we've come from – are the most effective stories of all. This is a powerful way to bring them to life."*

Stories help us connect with each other as human beings.

They're a great way to make lessons tangible and real.

Marketers understand that a brand has a story behind it, one that's meaningful to the customer. It's a story that creates a "point of difference" for the brand, something that makes the brand unique in the marketplace.

Before they hire you, they'll want to know your story. And if you don't have a story… well…

Here's what Lee Clontz, a University of South Carolina graduate, has to say about building your own story:

"The quickest way not to get a job is to bore an interviewer. Nothing is worse than a boring applicant. College is a tremendous opportunity to do different things, explore exciting options, and take interesting classes.

"Do something different, something impressive.

"Have an interesting story ready that will set you apart from the hordes of other people your interviewer will meet.

"Do something others aren't doing.

"You've got to build your story – something that tells us why you have a passion for the business, or lessons you learned, or the time you demonstrated leadership skills.

"A story about your talents, your initiative, or versatility.

"There's nothing wrong with an interviewer finishing up and thinking of you as 'that Peace Corps person' or 'the newspaper editor.' In a pile of résumés, you've got to be more than

just a name. To do that, you've got to be different, and you've got to be interesting."

Sometimes you build that story. Sometimes it just happens. Here's an example: The Potato Chip Story.

It comes from Chris Pultorak, a Temple graduate, who ended up at Foote, Cone & Belding (FCB) in Chicago.

"In college I interviewed for a combination scholarship / internship program that was being offered by a local advertising organization.

"Right in the middle of my interview, the four board members were delivered their lunch. Everything was fine until they realized the delivery guy stiffed them on their potato chips.

"I don't think they heard a single thing I said after that. I talked. They ate. They grumbled about not having potato chips.

"Then they nodded and thanked me for coming.

"On my way out, I noticed the next candidate waiting in the lobby for his interview. I also noticed a food vendor parked right in front of the building. So, I bought four bags of chips, handed them to the next candidate, and said, 'Here, they'll love you for it.'

"The next day I received a call from the review board awarding me the scholarship. And I became known as 'that potato chip guy.'"

This story positions Chris as that "potato chip" guy. It's short, but contains a beginning, middle, and end. Some dramatic conflict. A motif of potato chips throughout. And the simple surprise of the punch line.

Most of all, it tells us something about Chris. It tells us that he's observant, empathetic, that he has a sense of humor and can respond quickly to new situations with the right moves.

Sounds like the kind of person you'd want as an account executive, doesn't it? That's what a story can do.

How to Build Your Story.

Is there a key event or accomplishment that dramatizes your Brand You! personality?

How do you become "The _____ person?"

How you fill in that blank will start to define your brand.

This story should be yours and yours alone.

It should be organized and memorable.

While you're thinking, let's give you a few more insights about stories and narrative structure.

What Is a Story? Five Characteristics.

1. **Structure.** First, know the main structure. A story has a beginning, middle, and end. It usually flows through time.

2. **Motifs.** Second, a story has motifs – threads that wind their way through the story help it hang together so that, in the end, the viewer, listener, or reader can see a discernible pattern. The motifs can be repeated images or words, those central to the story's meaning.

3. **Drama.** Third, a story has drama. It may be conflict that is then resolved, but not necessarily. Usually, it's some action that rises and crests in the mind of the person on the receiving end. Went to meeting – disaster – no potato chips – they didn't listen to me – got them potato chips – I got the job.

4. **Anchor.** Fourth, a story has an anchor, which is its dominant meaning or theme. It is the single most important message you want remembered. The beginning, middle, end, motifs, and drama are tied to that anchor.

5. **Surprise.** Fifth, there's a bit of a surprise. If it's a joke, it's the punch line. There's, some sort of reward to the story that makes it worth remembering.

During and after a story is told to someone, that person should be able to condense it and wrap it into a tight package of meaning.

So, we ask again, what's your story?

Want to know the story for why I wrote this book?

Went to a "portfolio night," at a local university. *"Oh, this is going to be nice,"* I said to myself, expecting to see some nice, tight, well-presented portfolios.

I got there. Nice event. It was seniors and grad students showing me they were ready for the world. Nice hors d'oeuvres and small sandwiches. Beer, wine, soft drinks.

And then... I saw their portfolios. A wall-to-wall disaster.

Blah blah blah. Let me explain this.

Blah blah blah. Let me explain that.

No focus. Term papers disguised as case histories.

Over-written. No summaries. Blah blah blah.

"Let me tell you about my research..." Computer screens filled with unreadable type.

"Holy smoke!" I said to myself – actually it was a bit more rude than that, but you guys are young and impressionable.

"Holy smoke!" I said to myself, *"They don't have a clue!"*

And that's why I wrote *Brand You!* So you'd have a clue.

OK, that's my story. Time for you to get back to yours.

Challenge #2: The Brand You! Benefit.

By the time my "Why I Wrote This Book" story was over, you sort of knew why this book was in your hands – and you kind of knew the benefit. I wrote it to save you from being at the end of your college career – not ready for today's business world.

You know that I'm on your side and care about helping you find your own road to success – just like I found mine.

So what's your benefit? To them. We know the benefit to

you – a nice shiny new job. *What's the benefit to the target?*

You've got your target in mind.

You're working on some nice Brand You! slogans and graphics – what's the next problem we have to solve?

It's sort of that commodity/uniqueness thing.

The generic benefit – hiring a competent person who will help your business succeed – has to be combined with some sort of unique brand personality.

It doesn't have to be too tricky. It doesn't have to "over-sell" who you are and what you can do.

It does have to be *authentic.*

Let's look back at our last two brand stories.

The Potato Chip Guy – he sees a problem and handles it.

The *Brand You!* book – this book wants you to succeed in getting ready to get a job (funny how that last part of the phrase is the subhead).

OK, you know what you have to do. Let's do it.

Challenge #3: Your Brand You! Campaign.

Think politics. First, you need to enter the primaries. You'll do a bit of local meet and greet and establish yourself.

Then, as you identify the issues, and build name (brand) recognition, you begin to shape your national push.

Sound familiar? That's kind of how you have to do it.

You start local – learning the market, seeing what they want, and building your database.

Then you go after it: You have a portfolio that meets – or exceeds – expectations. You've identified some people in your network. Some are helping you. Some you're meeting for the second or third time.

You've got your "Hit List." Your Brand You! materials are now in their third, fourth, or fifth revisions. Right?

If at first you don't succeed...

OK, we don't start by making the All-Star Team. Most times we're lucky to just get picked.

Six years into the business, I became a VP/Creative Director at Leo Burnett. Yeah, youngest ever. Still, I think. Long time ago. Anyway... know what I put on my office door?

I posted a big – really big – blow-up of a rejection letter I'd received from the Leo Burnett Company in my junior year.

The rejection was for whatever the heck I had in my first or second portfolio. It was polite. And it was correct.

Because I didn't deserve to get hired for that portfolio. No way. It took me until the summer before my senior year – on that trip to New York – to finally see what the heck a winning portfolio was supposed to look like. At that point, I "got it."

Then, all I had to do was do the work. But I finally knew what I was aiming for. I finally had a clue. It took me a while.

All the more reason to get started now. Right?

The End of the Chapter. The Start of Your Campaign.

OK, here we go. Next, we're going to give you a few clues.

In the final section we'll be focusing on how to start building your portfolio – one of the things that will really help to define Brand You!

Let's close out here with some words from Tom Peters. They were contained in his very first article, "The Brand Called You," and a book he wrote about the same time, *Re-Imagine! Business Excellence in a Disruptive Age.*

Here goes...

Think Like an Entrepreneur.

"Even as you work for someone else, you should, in a good way, 'be the boss of your own show.' How you do your current job should enhance your market value."

Always Be a Closer.
  "As all true business people know. Life is sales.
  The rest is details."
Embrace Marketing.
  "You need to master much more of the marketing puzzle
  than you did in the past."
  "Market your point of view. Market your value."
Thrive on Ambiguity.
  "Mixed signals. Uncertain circumstances.
  Don't just 'deal with it.'
  Work to thrive in that environment
  – it could be with us for a while."
Nurture Your Network.
  "Loyalty is more important than ever."
  The old loyalty was vertical. Loyalty to a hierarchy.
  New loyalty is horizontal."
  "You must build – and deliberately manage
  – an ever-expanding network of professional contacts
  throughout your field."
Relish Technology.
  "You must instinctively appreciate the unequivocal fact that
  the internet and everything that comes in its wake will turn
  business upside-down in an astonishingly short period.
  The prospect should make you
  'tingle with joy and anticipation.'"
The Brand Called You.
  "It's this simple. You are a brand.
  You are in charge of your brand.
  There is no single path to success.
  And there is no one right way
  to create the brand called You.
  Except this. Start today. Or else!"

Things To Do:

OK, this one's easy-to-read. Doing it might take a while.

❏ **Your Brand You! Objective. Fill in those blanks.**

Target Industry.

**My objective is to get a starting job in
(Target Industry)** _____,

 and I will also take a look at:

Alternate Target Industry #1 _____,

Alternate Target Industry #2 _____,

and Alternate Target Industry #3 _____.

Target Geography.

**At present, the best place for me to look is:
"Best Bet" Market** _____

 But I'll also keep in mind opportunities in

Alternate Market #1 _____,

Alternate Market #2 _____,

and Alternate Market #3 _____.

❏ **Your Brand You! Personality.** Fill in the blanks.

 Remember, this is just a starting point.

 Pick a Word _____

 Pick another Word _____

 Pick a Phrase _____

 Pick a Goal or Dream (your BHAG) _____

 _____

 Say something funny (or insulting) about yourself.

 _____·_____

 _____·_____

 _____·_____

❏ **Differentiation.** Think about how to differentiate yourself – even though you're a bit of a commodity.

❏ **Your Brand You! Story.** Something else to think about. What do you like to do? Times you won. Lessons you learned. Problems you solved. Some brief anecdote from your past that kind of tells us who you are – and what it might be like to have you on the team.

Remember, *stories teach.*

❏ **Your Brand You! Campaign.** Start your engines. It's time to start thinking about it. And planning it. How about developing that early database and those early members of your network? Yes. Good idea.

V. Career Gear 3:
• (Your *Brand You!* Portfolio)

MANY THINGS ARE IMPORTANT. Some are *critical.* Your portfolio will be critical. Simply put, it's a measure of how you'll do the work – the work they hire you to do.

But getting it right isn't always simple.

Right now, you're in the process of acquiring the knowledge and ability that will make you qualified. But there's more.

You also need to know what the current standard is within the industry you're aiming at. Then you have to try and match – or, better yet – beat that standard.

Because you know that one other reality of the 21st Century marketplace is that a lot of people almost like you will be knocking on just about every door. That's just part of it.

You also need to know who to know.

This is not always easy. When you're in the middle of a college campus, it can be a little bit hard to find the ones you need to find – they're out there somewhere. But where?

That's why you need a network – to help you assemble the market intelligence you need to get smarter... and get rolling.

By the way, even though it's a tough job, putting together your portfolio may be one of the most enjoyable and satisfying things that you do in your college career.

Better yet, some of the people you will get to know as you build your network may become friends for life.

We call that a win/win.

23. Delivering The Deliverables.

LET'S DO LAUNCH! It's time to start organizing your very own Brand You! Campaign. Sure, some of these things aren't going to happen for a year or so.

But the sooner we start, the better we'll do. Right?

You also need that extra time in case there are some bumps in the road – like a shift of career focus, or a change of mind on where you'd like to live.

Hey, the sooner you know, the better you can deal with it.

Yes, a few are lucky enough to know exactly what they want to do and where they want to do it – but for most of us, it's a year or two process.

Putting It Together.

Let's start putting it all together. Every campaign is different.

Since each of us is a different product (Brand You!), and a slightly different market configuration (your target industry and your target geography). Naturally, the details will vary.

But most campaigns have these building blocks:

1. **Your Résumé.** (Or résumés for different targets.) On one page, you should be able to present, in writing, why you are qualified for an entry-level job at a company in your target. Rewriting it will make it better. We think it should have a photo. (Others may disagree.)

2. **Brand You! Graphic Materials:** Your 3-Up, current Brand You! graphic, and mailing materials. How about a graphic file that will make a letter from your computer look like stationery – for those cover letters you're going to write.

3. **Your "O.P."** Your Online Presence will start with a good LinkedIn profile – plus whatever else in Social Media makes sense. A Facebook page that you'll be comfortable being viewed by a prospective employer and whatever else you can add to boost your "O.P."
   Is it time for something extra? You might not be ready for your own video podcast yet, but what can you do? What can you put out there that's "BrandYou?"

4. **Your Database and Your Target List**. Names and addresses of the companies on your target list. Plus the people you should contact. Plus some information about them. How are you handling this? Do you have good codes – so you can find who you're looking for quickly? Remember that there's nothing wrong with "weak connections." Try to add names as often as possible.

5. **Your Brand Story.** How's that coming along? Got something you can try on friends? In a few comfortable sentences, you should be able to introduce and position yourself in a memorable way.

6. **Your Brand You Portfolio.** *The ultimate deliverable.* This shows everyone the kind of job you can do.

Planning Your Launch.

Those are the pieces you'll need. Then, it's time to put them into action. If possible, try to have enough lead time for some informational interviews and portfolio evaluations.

1. **The Roll-Out.** It's time to start to making the connections that will ultimately lead you to that first job – the first step on your career path. Let's give it a bit more strategic thought – what's your Target? How do you get rolling?

2. **Your Initial Contact Piece.** You need to start working on some sort of written communication you'll use to introduce yourself. It should work as both a letter – a "cover letter" – and as an email. What else should you include or attach? A résumé? I guess. Can we do better than that? Perhaps something that's a bit more "Brand You!" Tell them you'll contact them. Do it. It's not their job to contact you.

3. **Early Informational Interviews.** Start close and easy. Find the closest companies and let them know that your purpose is to know more about them. If some of these companies are out of town, try to do it during break or summer. And try to do it before your senior year, so you can have an interview without either you or the company being under pressure. Bring the early version of your portfolio.

4. **Follow Up.** You have to do what you say you'll do. Follow up and try to schedule some sort of initial interview. If possible, try to schedule an informational interview. Hey, maybe you need to do a company profile for a class project. Hmmmmm…

5. **Follow Up Your Follow Up.** Pleasant tenacity should be one of the skills you develop at this stage of the game. Try to project a feeling of being positive and organized – rather than a desperate nag.

6. **Feedback and Revisions.** Few of us get it right the first time. Find out what's working and what's not. Try to get a look at other successful portfolios. Once you see what the best looks like, it's a lot easier to make yours better.

And here's a preview of the rest of this book:

Portfolio. Portfolio. Portfolio. Portfolio.

Things To Do:

So what have you done so far? Let's keep going.

❏ **Your Résumé.**

❏ **Brand You Graphic Materials:** Brand icon. 3-Up. Got a business card yet? Brand icon for stationery?

❏ **Your "O.P."** Anything noteworthy?

❏ **Database and Target List.** Any names you want to follow up on right now?

❏ **Your Brand Story.** Got any good ones yet?

❏ **Your Brand You Portfolio.** Coming right up. Helpful hint: the more portfolios you see, the better you'll do – you need to know what the best looks like.

❏ **Roll Out.** Got a rough schedule yet? When?

❏ **Initial Contact Piece.** Got a cover letter? Got someone to send it to? How about your favorite instructor? For practice.

❏ **Informational Interviews.** Target the biggest player in your field. Study up on them. Schedule an interview. Can't go there? Do it by phone. Or send your questions by email.

❏ **Follow-up.** They don't call you. You call them.

❏ **Feedback and Revisions.** How do we make it better? Who can help us?

24. Portfolios. The Other Side.

BY THE TIME YOU'RE DONE, you will have spent an amazing amount of time on your portfolio. Every page, every paragraph – that 30-page plans book – all of it the result of a college education's worth of effort, learning, and accomplishment. We know that.

But now let's look at that process from the other side. How many people and portfolios, résume´s and LinkedIn profiles, good GPA's and relevant internships will they be looking at?

It gets better. During the first round, they're looking to eliminate. You simply can't carefully evaluate over one hundred candidates. So the first thing they have to do is get it down to a dozen or so. So, the first thing – details.

Details.

Remember, in the first round, everybody's looking for reasons to eliminate candidates. Mistakes are fatal.

Get the names right. Get the spelling right. To the best of your ability, know who will be reviewing your work.

When you send your portfolio, résumé. or cover letter, be sure you direct it to the right person, don't just address it "Dear Sir/Madam." Take the time to get it right.

If a prospective employer asks to see an online portfolio, make sure that's what you send, – not a PDF or a Word document. Make sure typefaces are consistent. No spelling mistakes.

Pay extra attention to the exact branding of the company. If there's an uppercase or a space within their company name, make sure you write it that way. Really.

It's worth repeating. At the first stage, companies look for reasons to cull the huge number of applications that hit their desk each day. Don't give them an excuse.

Quick Communication.

Today, we all swim in a media environment that's almost a white noise of messaging. Think about it. Your email box, a walk through a convenience store, the university course catalog, and the new menu at that nice new restaurant.

You see where this is headed.

Interviewers have to work their way through a ton of information. There's been some research done on how much time they spend per page – initially. Ready?

Somewhere between 2.5 seconds and 20 seconds.

Right, that piece that you worked on until 2a.m. is going to get less than 30 seconds the first time out. And what about that terrific insight that's buried on page 23 of the plans book? Hmmmm. Maybe it shouldn't be buried on page 23.

This is the point we need to make over and over. And over.

Those on the other side of reviewing your résumé and portfolio – very nice people – are very busy people.

From their perspective, it often gets to be a blur.

You need to differentiate and communicate the benefit of being someone they should consider quickly and clearly.

Differentiation.

This is one of the toughest of topics. If you are clean, clear, and well-behaved – how do you stand out among all the others who are just as clean, clear, and well-behaved?

And, if you take it just a little bit over the top, do they notice you and smile slightly as they toss your "out of the box" résumé into the circular file (i.e., the wastebasket)?

Quick question. What's your dimension of differentiation? What if your name is Susan Smith and you're applying for a job with the XYZ Corporation? What if you did just a bit of research and saw how you might be a good fit?

Why would you be a good fit? Your research tells you that XYZ has a tradition of service, a brand new technology product, and a Nebraska location. Let's put a two-page piece ahead of your portfolio. The first page looks something like this.

The second page – in quick concise bullet points – will tell us that you understand service. Remember, they don't teach that in school – tap into some summer jobs – something.

Then, a bullet point about your familiarity with their technology – and your enthusiasm for XYZ's product – assuming you can do that in an authentic way.

Finally, even though you're not a Husker, let them know you like Nebraska – assuming that its truthful. Get the idea?

Will you get the job with XYZ? Maybe. Maybe not. But we bet that this gets you past the first cut.

The point is – *see the process from the other side!*

Things To Do:

Try to add this habit to your Swiss Army Knife.

- **See Things from The Other Side.** As the legend goes, the famous ad executive, Bill Bernbach, kept a little piece of paper in his pocket. It said, *"Maybe he's right."*

25. Portfolio Principles:

THESE DAYS, JUST ABOUT EVERY STRATCOM JOB needs some sort of portfolio. We've collected as much up-to-date information on what should be in these portfolios as we could.

In some areas, like design and advertising creative, they've been using portfolios for decades. While portfolios have evolved over the years, the concept is well established.

In other areas, like research and account management, there is a shorter history and fewer examples.

For a start, let's cover:

• **Basic Portfolio Structure**

• **Portfolio Problems and Challenges** and…

• **Managing the Experience**

Then we'll cover a few other topics. Such as **Things You Can Put in a Portfolio** and an initial guide to what should be in various types of portfolios. Each is kind of a long "laundry list," which should be helpful as you build your own Brand You! presentation from the growing range of portfolio types.

The Purpose of a Portfolio.

To state the obvious, the overall purpose of a portfolio is to provide evidence that you are the one for the job.

In many creative areas, such as copywriting, art direction, design, and production, the portfolio remains the key judging standard of your professional skills throughout your career.

In other career areas, experience and professional accomplishment tends to replace the just-out-of-school portfolio, though it's my guess that case histories, presented along with a résumé, will become a larger part of everyone's career path.

For the moment, let's focus on the portfolio that helps you transition from the student side to the salaried side.

Simply put, *a portfolio is a collection of your strongest work presented as professionally as possible.*

Furthermore, for the student starting out, *your portfolio contains significant samples of your student work.* These should provide evidence of effort, skill, and achievement.

While we will end up taking you through a wide range of possible content, let's start with some basics.

Basic Portfolio Structure.

You may get an abundance of advice on how it should be organized, what should be included, and how to present it. A common phrase will be, "just show the work." As in, "don't waste my time with a lot of introductions and explanations."

We absolutely agree with the "don't waste my time" part of that advice. But the rest of that, in our view, needs a bit more management – particularly that all-important first impression.

We believe that, in almost every case, a portfolio – including yours – should begin with:

- **A Branded Title Page.** Who is presenting this portfolio? Again, let's not waste time, but let's begin by giving them something to remember – that conveys Brand You!

- **A Quick Bit of "Navigation."** What are we about to see? Can you get us ready for the ride? It could be a Table of Contents. It could be that your Branded Title Page is also your Home Page, so we'll see traditional navigation icons.

- **The Work – with Summary Intros.** Except for very obvious ad campaigns, most student projects need a brief bit of introduction. And most student introductions are w-a-a-a-y-y-y t-o-o-o-o l-o-o-n-n-g-g!

- We recommend that you put some sort of title page in front of each project – unless the title page itself does the job.

In some cases, the Summary Intro will be almost all you need. The entire project may still be there. But if you start by saying that your Zoo Who fund-raising Drive was the best ever – with a big Thank You from the Zoo Director, we may take a pass on the Baby Goat video, even though it got over 100,000 hits on YouTube. But you can tell us about it. Quickly.

A solid Summary Intro shows you what is there for review, but does not demand that a busy executive follow every step. Those who need to know the details will dig in. And now they know where to look. Others will move along – and appreciate that their time was respected.

- **A Résumé.** You have to have one – neat, organized, and easy to see what's important. This can be trickier than you think. For example, some want your experience first, while others want to know your software skills. There's still an art to making a great résumé. Our opinion is that a bit of visual on your résumé wouldn't hurt – and we are also in the "put a nice photo in it" category. There is debate – that's where we come out.

Why? Because it helps the interviewer . It's one less thing for them to process. Clear, quick communication.

- **Related Materials.** Don't put those poems essays, or works of art in front – but, if the work is good, really good, it may be worth including.

True story.

One of my last copywriting hires was Cal McAllister. He really didn't have a standard advertising portfolio. He was an associate editor at *Streetwise.* But when I saw a few of his pieces for his college newspaper, I saw that he could flat-out write.

Today, he's a co-owner of one of the top "New Wave" agencies. Everybody wants to work there. I hired him based on a bit of basketball wisdom, *"You can't teach height."*

Remember, the people who are hiring are looking for smart, talented people. If you have work that demonstrates that you're one of those people, well, maybe you can show it. But just the articles and short stories, please – not the novel.

Then, one of two things will happen.

Your talent will be affirmed as you get hired – or you just learned a valuable lesson – you're not yet as talented as you think. Or maybe you just interviewed with the wrong person.

A Quick Review.

For portfolios in general. You want…

- **A Branded Title Page.**

- **A Quick Bit of Navigation.** (Can be on the title page)

- **The Work – with Summary Intros.** (If appropriate)

- **A Résumé.**

- **Related Materials.** (Use restraint and good judgment)

Portfolio Problems & Challenges

Getting that first job can be challenging. Having a portfolio that "delivers the goods" is certainly key – but it's not that easy.

Once upon a time – when I was working on my portfolio, there was kind of a standard advertising portfolio. It was mostly print, you created "for instance" ads that stayed away from clients of the agencies where you were interviewing.

If you showed up with an ad for one of their clients, they closed their eyes, slammed the book shut, and told you to please remove it immediately – and maybe remove yourself as well.

There were all sorts of unhappy problems associated with people showing up with unsolicited work for current clients. But I digress…

The point is this. Back then, there was a fairly standard format – and the jobs were also fairly standard.

In advertising, back then, you started in print – maybe a bit of radio thrown in – to see if you were any good at it.

Then, maybe in a few years, you learned TV.

That was then. Today, here's the deal. Good news. Bad news.

Problem #1. An Explosion of Opportunity. As you know quite well – because you're living it – there's a wide range of skills needed in today's marketing world – and a wide range of opportunities: Viral Online. Social. Experiential.

It's a moving target. For example, think about the constant evolution of social media platforms.

That's good news because there are more things going on – and it's bad news because neither the jobs themselves nor what they're looking for are as standardized.

Problem #2. How Do I Deliver My Portfolio? Yes, you have many options. Online, on a disc or flash drive, or as a nicely printed package. Full color.

My suggestion is to develop the capability to deliver your portfolio in a fairly wide range of formats. That includes both an easy-to-access online version, and an easy-to-distribute and easy-to-navigate free-standing version – either printed or digital. Here are my thoughts on portfolio options:

- **Online.** You already have your URL, right? And you're on track to get your website up and running, right? If you don't, please put these items on your Things-I-Better-Get-Done-Very-Soon list.

- **CD or Flash Drive.** I'd recommend that you do more than write your name on it. If it's a CD, have a nice label, and – minimum – an insert. These days, packaging is one more dimension in which we compete. Make yours a winner. Flash drives are a bit more generic, but we're starting to find fewer CD drives, and everyone still has a USB.

I also have a few low-tech suggestions:

1. **Tape that flash drive to your business card.** Or maybe a Band-Aid - with something clever written on it.

2. **Fold up one of your 3-ups.** Turn it into a package. Write a note to the person who's getting it – or print up a promo version – with a mini-resumé. Tape your flash drive to that.

3. **Design a custom piece.** Big. Small. Whatever. Make it an extension of Brand You!

4. **A Printed Book, Mini-Book, or Traditional Portfolio.** Yes, I know that we're all wired in – but sometimes we like to sit with a hard copy in our hands and turn actual pages. In general, there are three types:

A. Custom-Printed. You could go all the way to one done by ShutterFly – or just have something from a copy shop. Comb-binding, or a binder with page protectors, dividers, and pockets for extra business cards and résumés.

B. The Mini-Book. If your entire portfolio has a lot in it, you might want to produce a smaller edited version – in quantity. Then you can do a nice direct campaign. But, be sure to individually address the recipients as best you can. Even the best portfolio addressed to "Dear Occupant" gets you off to a bad start.

C. The Traditional Portfolio. A case with a zipper. A folder that holds some presentation decks. A case that holds a whole multimedia bag of tricks. If you've got something special, you might want to consider making the packaging special, too. Art supply stores and office supply stores still have a lot of these types of packaging – do a bit of browsing.

And one more thing… the "Leave Behind." You want them to remember you. That means you might want to leave behind some examples. Consider distilling your portfolio into just a few pieces and printing up a few extra copies. You'll also probably want to add a bit of contact information as well. How can you make them remember you and keep what you left? Give it a thought.

Problem #3. The Interviewer May Be "Behind the Curve."
Once again, the good news is the bad news. One of the reasons the communications industry is constantly looking to hire new talent – particularly when it comes to contemporary creative content – is that both the media platforms and the content style are evolving.

This media platform evolution thing is new – getting it right is critical.

When I was hired, creatives in my generation had the task of telling the older generation what was happening in popular culture – particularly music. Now it's social media platforms – and music (though for the old stuff, we get to tell you). It can make the process more than a bit confusing.

Think about it. Who do you hire when you're not even sure what you're looking for? Yikes!

Problem #4. The New Poverty Class. Welcome to the world of the "Time-Poor." These days, if you're working, you are often extremely busy. As for the ones who are hiring because they need help? They're the busiest.

See where this is headed? Again. The people who first need to spend the time to see if you're the one they want to hire – and then spend some more time to teach you some of the things you need to know… very very busy.

Here's what Kimberly Easley, who reviews portfolios for VML, has to say, *"I have about four minutes to look at your entire portfolio, and decide in that four minutes. And that's if I like what I see when I first click on it. Think about what kind of impression you want to make. The first image must be phenomenal, if you're not proud of it, take it out."*

Yow! Four minutes. They're busy. We all are.

Oops. Got a meeting. Often, they say they'll get back to you – but they don't – not because they're bad people – they're just too busy. The ones that aren't busy? Did you really want to work for them?

So, just when you're looking for a sit-down where you can really learn something from those who just hired you – you may be on your own.

By the way, that interview that went so well… and they were going to get back to you… Don't wait. Do a follow-up on one of your 3-Ups. Maybe an email, too.

Problems #5 through #50. Other Things to Avoid. There are infinite varieties of this problem – but they're all pretty much the same – *things that need explaining.*

This can be particularly true when you're coming out of school. Hey, you're just learning things – which is pretty much what a student does.

So, we are so delightfully full of this new knowledge that it seems like a good idea to take them through that same enriching path we were on – and – let them know how hard we worked – and all we learned – and how wonderful it was - and…

Get a grip. If you bore them now do you think they'll hire you to bore them later? Three to seven words. Not thirty-seven paragraphs.

Whatever you did to edit it down… it's still too long.

We know. It took you a while to get there – and it's really nice that you got an A – but do you realize how much of this stuff those on the hiring side have to deal with?

So how is it you're going to use those first four minutes? (Don't worry, if they eventually get serious, you'll have more than four minutes.)

Got a research report that contains the answer to selling Mazdas to Millenials? Why not give them a Summary Intro? How about…

THIS RESEARCH REPORT CONTAINS THE ANSWER TO SELLING MAZDAS TO MILLENNIALS.

One of two things will happen. Those interested just might read the report (that secret better be in it – early on – in the Executive Summary), and the rest of the busy executives will put you in the all-too-rare category of someone who "gets it." Get it?

Better yet, why put it in a great looking binder?

Sure, we know you didn't have to do all that much extra when you finished the class project, but what's the real point?

The real point is you need to make a good impression on somebody who is seeing a lot of people with not much time for any of them.

If the binder looks good on the outside, maybe they'll be interested in what's inside – or at least pass you along to the Director of Research – who will probably read what's inside.

And, of course, it better be good.

Managing the Experience

This is an extension of Problems #5 through 50. You not only have to make it short and sweet, you also have to make it tight and right. This is not a skill they've taught you.

Let's think about this a bit. Jason McCann, who is a Group Creative Director at AKQA, and who has seen a lot of portfolios, says simply: *"Students should just think of it like a presentation and boil it down to its essence."*

Easy to say. Part of the problem is that it's taken you this long just to figure it out. Boiling it down to an even more edited essence is something that – years from now – you'll probably get good at. We hope. But right now – not so much.

Think of it from the Other Side of the portfolio review process – the reviewer.

"3 to 7 words – or 37 paragraphs? Yes, we know that every paragraph was lovingly crafted – often late at night – and – best of all – you got an "A." But really, what's the point of this item? Say that. Get to the point.

What is it you expect me to read? Think about the reviewer – buried in portfolios from people like you. How can you make this an enjoyable experience – one that makes him or her want to hire you? Use Executive Summaries. Respect the valuable commodity of their time and attention.

Why should I keep reading? Put in what I call "road markers." The head of account planning might want to read the whole brief AND the focus group notes. The other executives will probably be fine with the objective, the results, and the work that the research inspired. Maybe a 30-second video snippet. Maybe.

That means part of "Managing the Experience" is providing the clues and cues that let different executives manage to navigate their own journey through your work.

Creating mini-headlines, Executive Summaries, and what we call a Summary Intro is some of the most difficult kind of writing. But you have to try.

We've given you three examples so far – Susan's intro to XYZ Corporation, that silly "Zoo Who?" Summary Intro – and a headline suggestion – or a PowerPoint slide – that introduces a Research Report.

Yes, we know that this was not necessary when you turned it in to your teacher. But when you've got just a moment with this important person, don't you want to make the best impression possible? Thought so.

In the next section, we're going to serve up a few more examples in the hope that you'll start to get good at delivering your own engaging and persuasive Summary Introductions in your own portfolio.

Now what should we do? Let's review.

Things To Do:

This is important. You really need to understand all you have to do to end up with a professional, we'd-like-to-offer-you-a-job quality portfolio.

1. **Basic Portfolio Structure.** Again, these are the major sections of a portfolio. Time to start thinking about it.

   • **A Branded Title Page.**

   • **Navigation.** (Can be on the title page)

   • **The Work.** (With Summary Intros)

   • **A Résumé.**

   • **Related Materials.** (Anything, but it has to be good)

   Make a list. Check it twice.

2. **Portfolio Problems and Challenges.**
   Let's think about this…

   • **Target Audience.** Do you have a clear idea of the Target Audience for your portfolio and the kind of portfolio you need to develop for that target?

   • **Online Delivery.** Do you have a website URL platform to deliver your portfolio online?

   • **Alternate Delivery.** What other platform will work for you? Why?

• **Materials.** Visit an office supply store and/or an art supply store and see what physical items (folders, binders, etc) there are for possible use. Also – take a look online.

3. **Managing the Experience.**

• **Target Description.** How would you describe the Target Audience for your current career objective?

• **Alternatives.** Are there any alternative Targets?

• **Skills.** What skills do you need to demonstrate?

• **"Reader-Friendly."** How reader-friendly is your presentation right now? What are you going to do to make your portfolio even more reader-friendly?

26. Things You Can Put in a Portfolio.

THIS IS A LONG "LAUNDRY LIST" SECTION. But you have to start somewhere. We're going to review the range of things that could be in your portfolio, with a few tips on how to present them in your Brand You! portfolio.

The topics are all over the lot. We've simply put them in alphabetical order. In the next chapter, we'll discuss the different types of portfolios for different career areas and which items might work best. Then, it's up to you.

Advertising.

Portfolios began as an effective way for advertising creatives – art directors and copywriters – to demonstrate their skills.

The portfolio – evolving over the years along with skills and experience – remains key to advancing a creative career.

In advertising, the portfolio remains a measure of your market value. As your "book" gets better, either you get promoted - or you get a better job down the street.

In the beginning, the advertising was "forinstance" ads, student assignments, and whatever else seemed to make sense. As time went by, they contained increasingly polished and professional-looking work from the portfolio schools.

Today, entry-level portfolios look *terrific!*

At the same time, dramatic changes in the ad business itself have created a troubling contradiction.

The advertising portfolios are getting better at the same time that many aspects of the business are getting worse. The business is troubled – even though the work itself is – on judgment – rather good.

If you seek a career in advertising, go for it – but realize that there are many related careers that also offer rewarding creative opportunities. And remember, the competition will be powerful. Give it your best.

Portfolio Schools:
Are you familiar with them? You might want to visit their websites and become familiar with the quality of work done by people who are serious about building a career-ready portfolio.

Work That Works!

Advertising with Impact
- Auto Insurance
- Fashion
- Fast Food
- Mobile Apps
- Nutraceuticals
- Punch Cigars

Warning: Contents May Explode!

Here's a partial list of schools. Check them out:
- Chicago Portfolio School
- Creative Circus
- Miami Ad School
- Portfolio Center
- San Diego Portfolio School
- Savannah College of Art and Design (SCAD)
- School of Visual Arts (SVA)
- VCU BrandCenter

Awards.
You bet! Today, there are more contests than ever.

So, no surprise, more awards than ever. Still, it counts – and we're impressed. Sort of. What did you win?
- The One Show? Impressed.
- A local design contest. Somewhat impressed.
- A student competition. Maybe. Maybe not.
- A professional competition. Probably.

And, if it was the AAF/NSAC…

AAF/NSAC Regional Winner
(I'm in the 2nd row, 3rd from the Left)

Hey, congratulations, some of us know that the AAF/NSAC is a very tough competition. We also know that you really worked hard. But, then again, a lot of us don't know.

And did you really want us to read that whole plans book? And which pages were yours?

One more thing. The year you won – or the year you're going to win – do you realize how many other plans books and ad campaigns for that particular client show up? It's a blur.

So, we're glad you won, but please realize that you might not get quite the reaction you were hoping for.

Still, the AAF/NSAC does do a great job of teaching you to work hard, and – you'll like this – most winning team members win jobs in the industry.

"Brand You!" Title Page.

Are you ready yet? Is it good enough? If you can develop your own identity – and it doesn't look like an amateur did it – this is probably a good thing.

Having said that, use common sense. If you're looking for a corporate design job, easy on the high punk graphics.

A business-like job, like entry-level account management – well, there's nothing wrong with that title page having something that looks like a business card on it.

This could also be the Title Page of your portfolio. Looking good and differentiating yourself – probably a good thing.

In a perfect world, your Title Page should feature a custom Brand You! look and your tagline.

To state the obvious, it should all reinforce your career objectives. If you're more in the design space, you need to show off your skills, create your own awesome logo.

If you're more corporate, something that's clean, clear, and conservative will probably do just fine. In the business world, we let the designers do the designing. Not your job.

To Your Health

Brooke Adams
Strategic Communications
Healthcare & More
brooke@toyourhealth.org

You do want a strong tagline if possible – relevant to your career objective. Try to tell interviewers quickly who you are, what you offer, and that you can get to the point quickly.

Here are some simple examples (Don't worry, lots more where these came from – you'll do fine creating your own.)

Tagline Examples:
> **Account Management –**
> > *Ready to Manage the Tough Stuff.*
> **Account Planning –** *Got Insight?*
> **Advertising Copywriting –** *Write Side Up.*
> **Advertising Art Direction –** *Made You Look!*
> **Design –** *Designing a Better Future*
> **Digital –** *I Can Dig It.*
> **Direct –** *What I Really Want to Do is Direct.*
> **Event Management & Experiential**
> > *We Make Happenings Happen.*

Non-Profits – *Let's Make It a Better World.*
Promotion – *Hire One. Get Two Free.*
Public Relations & Publicity
   – *The Art of Strategic Connection*
   – *Let's Make Media Magic!*
Research & Consumer Insight
   – *This Little Girl Knows Big Data.*
Sports Marketing
   – *Just a Beginner. Already a Winner.*
Startups – *Pitch. Pitch. Pitch.*

See what those taglines do? In each case, they communicate that the person is focused on being successful in that particular area of marketing.

Making your message clear at the very beginning is very important. As they say, *"You only get one chance to make a first impression."*

Briefs.

Should you add project or Brief Notes? Use your head.

If you're looking for a job as an account exec, project manager, or account planner, of course.

Successful Briefs should be a part of your portfolio.

In fact, they should probably lead with them – using an appropriate Summary Intro, of course. Be brief.

Then again, if you're an art director, designer, or copywriter, keep it to a sentence – if that. If there is something that might be of interest, stick it in the back of that particular project.

Some Really Great Briefs!

Click Here For A Peek Underneath Some Great Marketing Thinking.

Well-written project descriptions that allow employers to understand the brief and constraints can be important – if it's related to your skills and the job you're looking for.

But remember, even though many things are true, they don't all have to be in your portfolio.

Case Histories.

Much of the work you will be presenting in your portfolio will be – in one way or another – a Case History.

Hopefully, a Case History with measurable results that actually gets implemented. But, more often, a nice letter from the Director of Marketing will be the best you can do.

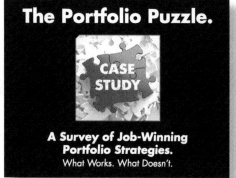

The Portfolio Puzzle.

CASE STUDY

A Survey of Job-Winning Portfolio Strategies.
What Works. What Doesn't.

But the BIG PROBLEM is that Case Histories can be big, deep, complicated documents.

That's the simple fact.

So what's the challenge?

By now, you see where we're going with this.

You have to do two things. First, you have to construct a clear and persuasive Summary Intro at the very front. Something that tells us what the Case was about, and gives us at least a clue as to what was learned and accomplished.

Second, you need to have an Executive Summary. Your answer is probably, "we already have one." No you don't.

Without having seen it, I will raise an eyebrow and ask a simple question, "Do you really?"

We are now talking about busy executives with a lot of other things on their minds – not the marketing director for whom the project was done, or the B-School professor who has been familiar with the project from the get-go and is kind of used to student-level work.

Remember, you're no longer selling the recommendation in the Case History. The playing field has changed.

Now the job is to sell them on _you!_

Coursework.

Maybe. If it's good – and it's work that is directly relevant to the career path you've chosen, that's probably appropriate.

But you really need to stay on topic. If you did work in a business course, and that's the area you're aiming at, that's fine. Likewise, Case Histories in your PR courses, and ad campaigns from your advertising courses – if they're good enough – they probably qualify.

However… if all you have to show is coursework, and the interviewers don't see a whole lot extra… don't expect enthusiastic response.

Why? Because you're sending the following message – you're not someone who "goes the extra mile."

As long as the work demonstrates skill and helps support your goals, it can be added. But if that's all there is, you may come up short when you're measured against those who've simply done more – in addition to the coursework.

Internships.

Sometimes these deserve more than a line or two on your résumé – particularly if your internship was in the same industry where you're looking for work.

It's hard to judge – but then again, it's hard to judge what your college degree means.

HOT!

I spent two years interning at one of Ohio's top design firms.

(I did a lot more than get coffee.)

Click Here & See What I Did.

So, if you learned something as an intern – with something to show for it – try to make it tangible in your portfolio.

Innovative Ideas.

Years ago, there was a guideline for advertising portfolios that was stated as "no science-fiction." That meant we didn't want to see ads for wild ideas that would never happen – like cars that drove themselves, or pills that enhanced your sex life.

The world changes, doesn't it?

Now, if you've got an idea for an app that will change the economy – or an industry – or a consumer item that will change our lives, well we're a bit more interested.

Some companies are more invested in cutting-edge technology than others. And you do need to realize that most of the jobs out there involve doing what other people want – not what you want. That said, the kind of fresh thinking that can think of a new snack food, a new computer application, or a brand new way to do the same old thing. Well, we're interested. Sort of.

So if you connect with the right people, it might work.

Meanwhile, the company that's interviewing you hopes that your portfolio has work in it that resembles the things they need done next week – and innovate to solve their problems.

Music.

Do you write music? Do you play? Being able to produce in the audio dimension is a specialty all its own, and if it's in your set of skills, you should let it be known.

Have you produced music? Performed on stage? Try to frame it so that it reinforces how well you can do the job for them. Like add music to a website – or be a great presenter.

It can be a line or two in your resumé – or it can be its own section in your portfolio. But be aware that if you make too much of a deal about it, the company doing the hiring may back off – because they know what you really want to do is go on the road and play in a band.

Photographs.

A decent "head shot" will add value to your portfolio and your résumé. Face value.

Today's mobile phones and iPads can deliver high-quality images, and there are plenty of young photographers looking for experience.

By the way, when you get your work professionally shot, the photographer may want a credit. If so, be sure to honor your agreement. This photo was done by my favorite photographer – Steve Ewert.

Presentations or Speeches.

These days, being able to present is a key skill. Certainly, your presence during the interview will provide some clues, but if you've been giving speeches or presentations to large groups – or doing video presentations – and you're fairly good at it – that's a point worth making.

This frame grab is from the iBook version of my copy textbook. You can also find it on YouTube.

Try to find a "souvenir" of your presentation – maybe a screen grab, or perhaps a poster or an invitation (create one if you must) and

The Viz Biz.

Brands. Celebrity. Technology.
A Brand New Era in Brand Advertising.
From The Copy Workshop Workbook - iBook

link to a short video excerpt – one that's both easy-to-access and easy-to-skip.

Remember, it better be good. No home movies!

Real Work You Did for Money.

This cuts both ways. You want to get hired for terrific work that's better than most "real" work. Then again, when you're just starting out, the projects they pay you for may be a bit "bottom of the barrel."

Recruitment manager Adele Leah advises: *"If you can, get work experience so you can include some commercial pieces in your folio. If you're finding it hard to get real world experience, set yourself mock briefs."*

My best advice – keep a grip on reality. If the work is a bit below what you'd like to be doing, let them know – without insulting your own work. Maybe something like this...

Research.

This will be interesting to many prospective employers – but you need to make it interesting. If they are smart and useful, you might include things like: a competitive analysis, focus groups, media audits, situation analysis, SWOT analysis (Strengths, Weaknesses, Opportunities, and Threats), or other examples of research conducted for strategic purposes.

That said, you need to hold to the standards of a solid Summary Intro or Executive Summary. Adding a little bit of "show biz" couldn't hurt. For example, grab a good verbatim from the focus groups for your Summary Intro.

"At our age, the favorite brand of automobile is 'used.'"

TOYOTA Focus Groups - AAF/NSAC

Self-Initiated Projects

Creative Directors like to see initiative. In fact, just about everyone hiring anyone likes to see initiative.

It might be work you did for a charity, a documentary, a music video, a children's book, or a book of poems.

You can let people know that you've done it as part of your portfolio presentation. But don't lead with it.

Then again, to state the obvious, your projects should be viewed as worth doing and of good quality.

Self-initiated projects can be a great way of showing off your creative thought processes and what you can do. It's also a great way to show what you're passionate about.

Your projects can be anything from an art installation, to a competition entry, to an exhibit, a 'zine, a pop-up store, a short film or some personal branding materials.

Here's a project I did just because I wanted to do it...

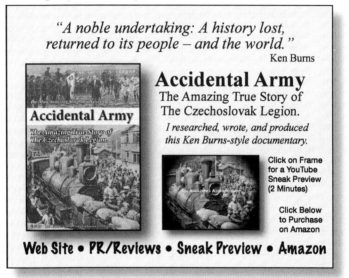

This is a 47-minute Ken Burns-style documentary on a topic that almost nobody ever heard of. In fact, I called it, *"The most amazing story you never heard."* It's *Accidental Army,* and it's actually kind of cool. At least that's my opinion. (Ken Burns liked it, too.)

Don't expect anyone to watch the whole thing, but give them options – like a YouTube Preview.

Social Media

If you have any active (and relevant) social media accounts, include them! That's all part of your "OP," your online presence.

But if one of your skills is managing social media, that's something else again – because social media expertise is one of the new skills that's of great interest to almost every marketer.

There are sites for social media specialists. You should track them down and consider maintaining a presence on industry-specific social media accounts, such as GitHub for developers, and Dribble and Behance for designers.

Everybody's on LinkedIn, and you should be, too – but it's not particularly defining. Likewise, feel free to include Twitter, Tumblr, etc., as well. Just so it's relevant — and you don't mind potential employers/clients seeing it.

Finally, always be prepared for clients/employers to look you up on Google. (We can 90% promise that they will.)

Startups.

Today, the entrepreneurial spirit is celebrated. Better yet, there's a whole infrastructure of venture capitalists, incubators, and KickStarter funding. Magazines like *WIRED* and *Fast Company,* are chock full of success stories.

If you can add a small piece of a big idea to your portfolio, have at it. And good luck.

However, we will add this one caveat – *confidentiality.*

We know you want to publicize your great idea, but if there are still some issues pending with the "IP," (Intellectual Property), you might need something like this frame.

And then, as you move ahead, you're probably going to need an actual confidentiality form. (PS. Good luck!)

Videos.

Yes, if they're good. No if they're still works in progress or need too much explanation – like explaining production problems, budget problems, or….

Once upon a time, enthusiastic amateurs made a good impression on us – because – back then – getting video shot and edited was complicated and expensive.

Ever Wonder What Happened To The Austro-Hungarian Empire?

Czech It Out!
Accidental Army: The Amazing True Story of the Czechoslovak Legion.

Today, it's different.

There's better equipment that's very affordable, and many more opportunities to gain experience and learn to work to a professional standard.

Hold that thought. And here's one more factor.

You really need to understand the video production being done by those with whom you're interviewing. It they make a living doing corporate training, don't expect an experimental music video to carry the day. Meanwhile, that cutting-edge video house may not get worked up about the documentary.

Be smart and professional. Knowing what *they* are looking for is certainly a step in the right direction.

Volunteer Work.

Volunteering your services says a lot about you. It can also be a smart move – if you can connect with a non-profit that offers opportunities to learn.

Fundraising can teach you a ton about direct marketing and event marketing. Work done for churches, charities, and local political campaigns? You bet.

My first year in the business, I volunteered for a local political campaign. I showed up and said, *"how can I help?"*

196

By year three, I was in charge of brochures and other materials for a bunch of independent candidates. I kept it up.

It was fun. Made friends with people all the way up to a US Senator. Six years later, the Governor of Illinois appointed me to the Illinois Arts Council and – ten years later – I had a run as Creative Director for a President of the United States.

No kidding. For that one, they paid me.

And it sure does look nice on the résumé. No kidding.

When first starting out, you'll probably work for free. That's okay, you have to start somewhere. And some of it may end up being the best stuff in your portfolio.

Just make sure you're doing work – or getting experience – that will help build your skills – and your portfolio.

Web Design.

This is important. Whether it's your own website – featuring your online portfolio, or whether this is one of the skills that you have to offer.

Either way, the most important thing in site design is usability. Can a person come to this site and "get it?"

Can they navigate the site without becoming confused?

Is it quick, clear, and easy? If the answer to any one of these is "no," you need to rethink your design decisions.

If you can demonstrate simplicity and clarity, as well as good design, that is a definite advantage.

Think "user-friendly."

In the example on the next page, SEO consultant Gary Le Masson makes his portfolio/résumé look like Google search results. The site is simple, clever, and makes his point clearly.

Better yet, it is perfect for the clients he's going after – people who want to rank high in Google search results.

Take a look…

The other example is much more complicated – it supports our advertising textbook company. We "backed up the truck."

- A bookstore with ecommerce (PayPal and 20% off)

- An Ad Museum (links to other ad history websites)

- A Study Hall (with Vocabulary and practice tests)

- An AdBuzz theater (with imbedded TV spots)

- A Jukebox (Mercury Award-Winning radio spots)

- MediaBuzz – support for *Strategic Media Decisions* plus a Workbook PDF you can download. FREE!

- Finally, there's CAFÉ – with a *ton* of useful PowerPoints, a few more teaching resources and downloads, plus a few more videos.

It's more complicated – but you "get it" in a moment.

BTW, the platform needs an update – it was done way before Flash and Java – but the visual design makes a complicated job fairly simple and easy-to-understand www.adbuzz.com

Things To Do:

Go directly to the next chapter...

27. Twelve Kinds of Portfolios:

THESE DAYS, EVERY STRATCOM SKILL POSITION needs some sort of portfolio. We've collected as much up-to-date information on what should be in these portfolios as we could.

As we said, some areas, such as design and advertising creative, have used portfolios for decades. While they're still evolving, the concept is well established.

In other areas, like research and account management, there's a shorter history and fewer examples. Still, with companies needing new hires to "hit the ground running," some sort of demonstration of job-ready skills is now more and more necessary in every field.

Since it's not as common for those who work outside the field of visual communication to have a portfolio, creating a collection of your work can help you stand out from your competitors, and demonstrate your initiative and organizational skills.

Here are the Twelve kinds (There is some duplication, like Account Planning/Research and Advertising Media/Media.):

- Account Executives
- Account Planning *(See Research & Consumer Insight)*
- Advertising Creative & Design
- Advertising Media *(See Media)*
- Digital, Direct, and Database
- Event Management & Experiential
- Media
- Nonprofits
- Promotion
- Public Relations & Publicity

- Research & Consumer Insight
- Social Media
- Sports Marketing
- Startups

This is our current compilation of initial good advice for portfolios in these various fields. Since portfolio development in many of these new career areas is still a work-in-progress, be sure to extend your research on the topic of what it takes for a winning portfolio in your chosen career area.

That said, here's our best advice at this time. And if you have better advice, please send it to us.

Account Executives.

Here's a basic format for account executives. It also works for other managerial-type job descriptions. Think of your portfolio as having four or five sections:

1. A "Brand You!" Title Frame

2. Your Résumé

3. Accomplishment Summaries

4. Other Relevant Materials

5. Topics of Personal Interest

John Minnec
Account Management

Ready To Handle The Tough Stuff!

Now let's cover these in more detail.

1. **Portfolio Title Frame:** Your name, logo (this can be fairly conservative – business card-style) with optional tagline.

2. **Résumé:** We recommend introducing it with a Summary Intro that can include a key accomplishment and a third-party validation – such as a quote. The focus of your résumé should be on key accomplishments. Quantify if possible.

   At the very least, provide good qualitative results. Include a visual where possible. Yes, that's right. Visuals may include graphs, tables, or charts. People are visually motivated; powerful visuals are used to stimulate the buyer for every product or service worldwide. Why shouldn't you do the same to generate an interview?

3. **Accomplishment Summaries:**
   These are one-page summaries of key accomplishments you have achieved throughout your career.

   Place each summary on its own page, though you can have an index in front if you feel some navigation is in order. Each Summary Intro can then be followed by the entire report or Case History, but the summary should be able to stand on its own.

   The Summary Intro should include a clear, descriptive title and indicate what was accomplished in a clear and positive way. If you think you can do the whole thing on one page, then you'll want the following:
   • A brief description of the problem or situation
   • A bulleted list of your actions
   • A summary of the results
   • Third party validation – if any
   Otherwise, settle for a Summary Intro and then present the more detailed assembly of material – which probably resembles the Case History presentation.

   Some recommend you develop as many as ten of these summaries for use in different situations.

That's good advice if you happen to have them. Then again, you'll typically only include three to five of them. So let's get those right.

Some Summary Advice. Go Backwards!

This is important. For the purposes of your portfolio, you may need to tell your stories *backwards*.

Until now, you're probably used to talking about these cases beginning with a "here was the problem" type of opening.

Remember, *you have no time.* Hiring decision-makers read résumés quickly – *between 2.5 and 20 seconds on average!*

Now you know why you need to grab their attention by giving away the ending first. You must communicate quickly!

Use this sequence: Result > Action > Situation.

Keep your accomplishment stories brief. One expert recommends about two sentences. Do it in as condensed a manner as you can. You'll get better as time goes by.

Truth in Résumés.

By the way, it shouldl go without saying, but be extra sure you are totally truthful about the accomplishments you list on your résumé. Have you really accomplished all the things you say you did? Should others also receive credit?

Remember that a résumé is a statement of facts.

While it is acceptable to put a spin on your accomplishments, the bottom line is that they all must still be truthful statements.

And don't think people won't check. HR directors are used to seeing the truth getting stretched in a résumé. They check.

And the only thing worse than people finding out about untruthful résumé statements beforehand is their finding out after you got the job.

This sort of thing can be grounds for dismissal.

A Cautionary Note.

This is worth repeating. Get to the point. Undisciplined PowerPoints cause genuine damage. Too many bullet points or too much type on a single frame results in "Death by PowerPoint."

I saw one example posted as a model portfolio, featuring small type and impossible-to-read documents.

I didn't bother to read further. Remember...

They're busy.

They've never seen the material before

They're looking for reasons to *eliminate* candidates.

Hold those thoughts.

4. **Other Relevant Materials:** Today's career descriptions are increasingly varied. Entry-level jobs are often more like Project Management jobs.

   Were there any other projects you managed? A fundraiser at school. Club activities that were interesting, successful, and well-attended.

   How about summer jobs or internships that taught you something important? Now that you've covered the business basics, you can provide further information that might make you someone they would want to hire.

5. **Topics of Personal Interest:** Again, once you've made it past the business stuff, a company that's thinking about hiring you wouldn't mind knowing a bit more about you as a human being.

   This very last section – which is optional – can be as personal as you want. Did you play on a team? Do you golf? These days, many jobs have a social aspect. Your prospective employer won't say it up front, but it is one of the things they'll bring into consideration during the final stages of a hiring decision.

So, is there anything else about you that a company might find useful and advantageous? If so, find a way to add it at the end of your portfolio.

Advertising Creative & Design

The tradition in advertising – for good reason – is to hire "creatives," primarily art directors and copywriters, based on their portfolio – aka your "book."

Today, as advertising's creative tactics expand into a wider variety of media channels – the portfolio is still the main hiring criterion – but what's in it has exploded!

The best agencies expect your portfolio to match the skill set, industry knowledge and creative surprise they need on a daily basis. And they need it now.

They'll usually want it online, and if the person making the hiring decision wants to see it another way, well your portfolio should be in that format as well.

Here are some portfolio tips and resources:

Resource #1. This book.
It's called *How to Put Your Book Together and Get a Job in Advertising.* Though it was first written in the previous century, a lot of the advice is timeless. It's also a lesson on how to communicate. Maxine Paetro, the author – now a co-author with James Patterson of best-selling novels – gives you solid get-started advice.

You may have to dial up the technology in today's job-winning portfolio – but the basic advice is still good.

Resources #2 & #3. These books.

Two other books claim to help. They probably do, because they really do help you learn what's involved. There's *Breaking In: Over 130 Advertising Insiders Reveal How to Build a Portfolio That Will Get You Hired.* This one gives you an idea of the range of opinions and standards in the industry.

Creative portfolio evaluation is often a very personal and subjective thing. Here, you get 130 different looks at it.

The other is *Pick Me: Breaking in to Advertising and Staying There* by "Jancy," Nancy Vonk and Janet Kestin, two top-flight Canadian creatives (they also had a lot to do with that wonderful Dove advertising). Both books are packed with good advice.

A little learning helps. And all that advice is nice. But the real bottom line is you have to do the work – and it has to be good. Make that exceptionally good.

What do you need in your physical book?

Simply put, work that works.

Advertising portfolios should have examples that are smart, distinctive, and – on judgment – effective.

Agencies look for eye-catching and creatively surprising pieces that highlight your ability to:

1. Think strategically.

2. Communicate complex concepts.

3. Utilize multiple current software applications... and

4. Solve real-world problems as part of challenging client objectives.

Your portfolio should also include: a brief biography, full résumé, and contact information.

Branding Your Book.

The pieces in your portfolio will show how you create and position brands for clients. The portfolio, in its entirety, will convey your own personal brand.

We are somewhat reluctant to give definitive advice in this category, since those hiring are often looking for those who break the mold.

The only additional advice we could offer is that this is one of the most competitive categories, and you must might want to consider some post-graduate work at one of the many excellent portfolio schools.

On this page are two examples of the quality of work that comes from the portfolio schools. Very good. Very competitive.

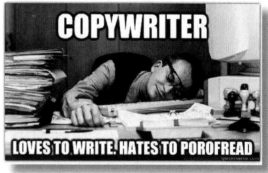

...& Design

Design Schools are already very well organized to help their students develop an excellent design portfolio.

That said, you might want to see what they do.

As design becomes an increasingly important part of all business strategy, integrating design concepts – such as *user experience* – into all of your work can make a lot of sense.

Advertising (Media)

Media has become one of the newly and truly creative areas of strategic planning. We'll cover it in a later portfolio section that we've cleverly titled, "Media." You'll find it under "M."

Digital, Direct & Database

The technologies in these three areas are all interrelated. That said, those who do the hiring are often very different people – and very different companies.

These can range from cutting-edge digital shops to the more traditional companies in direct.

All these companies are using the latest technology, and those with skill in this area should find themselves with a lot of interesting opportunities to choose from.

John Militello, now Director of Marketing Innovation & Strategy at Volvo, former ECD at Google, and also a professor at the School of Visual Arts, is the kind of person you want to impress in the digital arena. Here's his advice for students looking to build a cohesive portfolio in the digital space.

First, think about the human target and what service you can provide them. John says: *"We want students to go beyond this idea of integration and ask, 'What purpose does this provide the user, and what can I do to make the user's life better?' and then get deep into the brief."*

aaronyelton@digitalone.com

He wants to see thinking like this: *"What is that digital behavior that can help us come up with the creative so that it's a sound creative strategy? That's how you can go deeper and think before executing."*

Here's a digital portfolio tip: Quantify your experience, because it demonstrates your value in specific terms. Examples could be:

- *"My new homepage design helped increase time spent on page by one minute."*

- *"Landing page redesign dropped bounce rates by 15%."*

- *"New blog layout increased pages per session by 20%."*

There are different ways you can do this. The important thing is quantifying and showing results. You need to demonstrating that you are doing this for the human beings on the other side of the screen.

Direct & Database

Big data is the next big thing. At least this week.

But the long-term fact is that as our digital infrastructure is able to generate, collate, and correlate increasing amounts of data, those who can negotiate this world clearly and comfortably will be much in demand.

Your Skills and Technical Expertise.

This is what prospective employers will want to know about. In addition to communicating the benefit and results of your projects, they will be deeply interested in the details of what you know.

Your Challenge.

Your challenge will be to communicate what you know to those who very much need your services. However, in many cases, they will not know what you know.

If the person hiring you is up to speed, the two of you should connect. If you see clearly what's involved, move forward. *If you do not see clearly, proceed with caution.*

Leading Edge/Bleeding Edge.

Current data shows that 55% of big data projects are never completed! This finding was repeated in a second survey, that also found that the majority of on-premises big data projects aren't successful.

So what's the problem with big data? At the front end of many technologies, it is very common to find yourself not on the "leading edge," but, rather, on the "bleeding edge."

Be careful. The challenge in designing and presenting your portfolio in this very much in demand area is to be understandable. Then, you need to be sure those who hire you understand.

Meanwhile, much traditional database and direct work is profitable and growing, as those with big databases are discovering that they can do even more with their data.

In this area, we recommend one more qualification for that important first job.

Get hired by those who know what they're doing.

You may or may not remember the initial rollout of ACA, the Affordable Care Act (i.e. Obamacare). It was a disaster!

Then, some people who really knew what they were doing were brought in and got things on track.

You want a job with the second group – not the first group. So… how do you tell which is which? Good question.

That's why, in this category, we say proceed with caution.

You really want to start off working with the right people.

Interested in a Short Engagement?

S A L L Y   S N Y D E R

Engagement, Event, and Experiential Marketing.

Event Management & Experiential

There is a new and exciting emerging sector in the marketing playing field. It has a number of names "engagement marketing," "experiential marketing," "event marketing," "on-ground marketing," "live marketing," or "participation marketing."

Basically, it's a marketing approach that directly engages consumers. and invites and encourages them to participate with the brand in some appropriate and meaningful way.

For example, the Seattle Sounders' marketing agency, Wexley School for Girls (yes, that's their name) thinks of itself as a "fan factory." Sounders fans march to the stadium and respond to the call, "Scarves Up!"

Rather than looking at consumers as passive receivers of messages, engagement marketers believe that consumers should be actively involved in the production and co-creation of marketing programs, developing a relationship with the brand.

Engagement happens when brand and consumer connect. You've probably experienced it on campus, and if this is a type of marketing that appeals to you, it might be an area for you to explore. Explore is a good word – because you may have to go looking.

But not far, because there are already a number of these marketers already on your campus. Track them down, and there's a pretty good chance you can get some experience.

The Next New Thing.

This is a good example of the modern marketplace – with new fields growing, as older, more "mature" categories slow down.

You may have had a short segment on this type of marketing in a survey course. Or not. It's all pretty new.

So what do you do? You look, search, study, and, in the course of doing your regular coursework, you see if you can develop enough knowledge and enough examples to have your own unique Event Marketing portfolio.

Or your Experiential portfolio. Whatever.

Along the way, you'll learn who the pioneers are. You might even do some work for them – since a lot of engagement, event, and experiential happens on campus – not in the classroom.

An Engagement Marketing Menu.

Here are the types of activities that are regarded as engagement, event, and/or experiential. As you can tell, there's quite a bit of cross-over. The key is creating a connection.

Many of these activities – like blogs, email, mobile, and social marketing would also qualify in other categories.

What you'll find, more and more, are clients and suppliers who are "marketing agnostic" or "media agnostic."

That means their beliefs aren't tied to just one type of marketing tactic. They examine the marketing problem and develop solutions based on good judgment and an awareness of all the opportunities available.

Here's a list – in alphabetical order:

- **Blogs:** For engagement marketing purposes, companies can share content on their own blogs and participate as a commenter or content provider on relevant external blogs. Hosting a campaign that gives prizes to the readers of external blogs for their participation in some kind of contest is an example of engagement aimed at external blogs.

- **Crowdsourcing:** Crowdsourcing sites offer engagement marketing opportunities through their open media contests. Sites like these generate brand ambassadors as a byproduct of the process.

- **Events:** It may be called event management, or event marketing, or PR, or publicity. This is big business in virtually every market. Concerts. Street Fairs. Theatrical Events. Etc. Many unique suppliers and vendors participate.

- **Marketing through Amenities:** Here's one you might not have thought of – for example, a sponsored changing station.

- **Street Marketing:** Also known as "street teams," this involves marketing or promoting products or services, in an unconventional way, in public places. A related field is "ambient marketing" which uses other semi-public places, such as shopping centers. Street marketing involves the application of multiple techniques and practices in order to connect directly with customers – or potential customers. Two goals of this interaction are to generate an emotional reaction in the clients (Scarves Up!"), and to get people to remember brands in a new and different way.

Street Marketing for MICROSOFT from Wexley School for Girls.

Here's another early example from Wexley – a six-story "Big Ass Phone" introduction in New York for Microsoft. You can access the video at http://www.wexley.com/work/microsoft

- **Youth Marketing:** Also known as entertainment marketing, it tends to focus on popular events and activities that attract this target group.

- **Mobile Marketing Tours:** Often, brands will utilize custom-branded RV's, buses, and motor coaches to draw attention to their offering, serving as mobile billboards, as well as mobile centers to create brand experiences on-site in retail parking lots or at larger events.

Engagement marketing commonly uses tools such as:

- **Social Networking Sites:** Facebook, LinkedIn, and Twitter are ideal for engagement marketing.

These social media platforms provide a way for people to interact with brands and create a two-way dialogue between customers and companies. Most companies maintain a presence on several of these sites.

- **Webcasts:** While internal webcast meetings are intended for a small, specific invitation list, engagement marketing online events are aimed at a broader public audience. They are typically available live or on-demand, which allows viewers to view content on their own schedule. Similar to conferences, audience members can ask the speakers questions and participate in polls during live webcasts.

- **Email campaigns:** This is one of the earliest online engagement marketing tools, and, done well, they can still be tremendously effective and economical. Email marketing requires target audiences to opt-in to directly receive a marketer's emails.

Media

We live in a media age. For this section, let me tell you a story. It will help you understand how the whole thing is changing.

The Bushel Basket Story.

A few years ago, I was invited to attend a Career Day at the Chicago Portfolio School. This particular group of smart, eager students was in from the University of Georgia.

One of their graduates spoke. She was a very successful media professional who had graduated about ten years earlier. She took us on a quick tour of her career.

It was very varied. She'd been part of the revolution going on in the media world. She'd gone from an ad agency media department to a new media startup, to expanding online channels for existing media properties.

Clearly, she was very comfortable in this new business environment. Any questions? Per usual, no questions. (You guys really need to learn to ask questions when you have a chance.)

So I asked her one. It was about "bushel baskets."

I told her that I looked at media as bushel baskets. *"You've got your advertising budget and the media folks assign various amounts to various 'bushel baskets.'"*

"You assign a certain amount of the budget to the TV bushel basket, another chunk to the online bushel basket, and maybe a bit to your out-of-home bushel basket.

"And there seem to be new bushel baskets popping up all the time." She nodded.

So, I said, *"You've had a very successful career moving through this constantly changing world of media.*

Caroline Chen   Media Person

Big Ideas By the Bushel!

What would be your advice to these students here as to the road to success in media?"

She nodded her head again and thought for a minute. Then, she gave us her career advice. *"Invent a new bushel basket."*

Makes you think.

Here's another story about media.

Robert Pittman wasn't a whole lot older than you when he found himself working at the NBC station in Chicago. (He was a bit older when he had this picture taken.)

He was working on a late night show that featured something brand new at the time. Music videos.

The show was popular.

But wait, there's more!

Musical groups were coming up with new videos all the time. It was media that was new and exciting. Cable TV was also relatively new back then.

Pittman gave it a little more thought. Then he went and invented MTV!

These days, things like that can still happen in the brave new world of media. Brand new bushel baskets.

Extensions in The Media Age.

Now let's give a thought to media guru Marshall McLuhan.

Remember his concept of "extensions?"

McLuhan observed that media extends our senses, our awareness, and our knowledge. That's kind of interesting.

The revolutionary digital shift has enabled an almost infinite combination, recombination, and creation of media channels and products. Our media habits are changing.

For those reasons and more, people who want to work in tomorrow's media world will need an interesting combination of skills:

- **Traditional Media Skills.** You need to be good at math and statistics. Good attention to detail. These abilities are still important – particularly if you want to work at one of those big media planning and buying groups that are affiliated with agencies. (Still a good entry level job.(

- **New Media Skills.** As the media world changes, these are becoming increasingly important. You'll need to be up-to-date on the changing world of New Media.

- **Selling and Negotiating Skills.** If you're involved in buying or selling media, you need these abilities. Media sales is still a big entry category. It's tough, but if you're good at it, and represent a "hot" media property, you can do very well.

- **Cross-Media and Creative Packaging Skills.** Think Robert Pittman and MTV. Think about all the new media properties that are growing across media channels. Think about new "bushel baskets." Pretty exciting.

- **Social Sciences and Anthropology.** Think "connection planning." It's more important than ever to understand the new and changing media behaviors. As DDB Chairman Keith Reinhard observed, *"Today's toughest question is how to find your customers at the most strategic time – that's why media is the new creative frontier."*

- **Creativity in various aspects.** You may be involved in a startup - creating or developing new media channels and/or new media content.

When you add it all up, a lot of interesting things can go into today's media portfolio. Enjoy the ride.

NonProfits

Successful work in the nonprofit field involves a number of marketing disciplines: Cause Marketing, Database and Direct Marketing, Event Marketing, and Publicity.

They all need to work together to help your nonprofit meet its ongoing objective of fulfilling its specific mission while, at the same time, raising the funds needed to keep it going.

The good news is that it's fairly easy to get internships, and develop class projects, in the nonprofit area.

After all, they need help on an ongoing basis.

So, as you develop your nonprofit portfolio, you can probably generate good ex-

Smart. With Heart.

Carol Williams
Northwestern University

Adding Value to NonProfit Marketing

amples. Here are some of the topics and approaches that might be part of a successful nonprofit portfolio:

- **How You Made the Evening Special.** All groups have fundraisers. What did you do to make this one attractive and successful?

- **Raffle and Auction Success.** These are regular parts of fundraising events. Did you help yours make extra dollars?

- **Broadening Your Mission Message.** Does your nonprofit have outreach programs? Is there a way they do something extra in the community? Was there any publicity on these extras to enrich your nonprofit's message?

- **Extra Value/Extra Savings.** Yes, you often have to spend money to make money, but were you extra smart about it? Chicago Shakespeare Theater had their gala in the theater itself, and used existing props to dress up the evening while keeping expenses down.

- **Demonstrate Dedication.** Sometimes, you just have to keep at it. Fundraising by phone can be like that. It's one more piece of "added value" that people will look for. Yes, it's nice when you are delightfully creative. But sometimes, they will need people who can "grind it out." It won't hurt for you to demonstrate that you are that kind of person.

- **Leverage relationships.** Whether it's Board Members, vendors, or just good friends, making new and effective connections can often be a critical part of developing new programs. Perhaps someone is related to a band or group of entertainers that can be a low-cost (or free) part of your event. Someone may have access to a new list of people who might be interested. An exciting new venue – a restaurant, club, theater or gallery, might be the setting for a successful event. Sometimes it really is "who you know."

Promotion

Or do you say Sales Promotion? This remains a strong and important segment of marketing activity.

Brand. Buyer. Behavior. Benefit. Budget.

Your portfolio should demonstrate how you manage the "Five B's" of Promotion. The key is developing an incentive program powerful enough to stimulate buying behavior.

Simply put, you need to demonstrate results.

The purpose of a sales promotion program is to deliver short-term results – preferably results that are quantifiable.

Most school projects are advertising, publicity, or PR-oriented.

If you're serious about sales promotion you might want to focus on projects that have a bit more of a sales promotion characteristic. For example...

WE BEE READY!
- Brand.
- Buyer.
- Behavior.
- Benefit.
- Budget.

The Bee Team: Promotions That Perform!

Here are the kinds of projects that Sales Promotion firms might be interested in:

- **Booth at a campus fair** – Add up the number of email addresses collected – with a follow-up email offer that delivers a high value coupon by email.

- **"Cause Marketing."** Help organize an event – like a walk-athon. Measure participation and the money raised.

- **Concept Boards.** These would be initial ideas for possible promotions for a client. Sales promotion firms are idea-generators – they are always looking for more "idea people" who understand promotion.

- **Local Promotion.** Develop something for a campus pizza place or restaurant. Measure the traffic increase and numbers of coupons redeemed. Hopefully, there will also be a measurable sales increase. See if the restaurant owners will let you "crunch the numbers."

- **Promotional Item.** How about a T-shirt? Get something done for a campus concert. See if a local radio station wants to get involved. Be sure to include photos of students wearing that T-shirt. Or how about a bumper sticker?

- **Sampling Event.** What can you create? Experience all that's involved (it can be complicated) and measure the results.

- **Spring Break Promotion**. This is often a campus "hot button." Plan a Spring Break-related event. Promote it.

See what's going on here? It's fun – and it works!

Try to find out more about what the sales promotion firms in your area are like and what they work on. (They may call themselves something else.)

Intern if you can.

Try to put a sales promotion spin on your projects.

Public Relations & Publicity

Since so much of the public relations and publicity function now gets done online, you will need to deliver your portfolio in both an online version and a professional printed version.

You might also want to have it available as a PowerPoint.

In general, the PR portfolio is a collection of your best work presented to good advantage.

If you can demonstrate a specialty or focus in a certain segment of public relations – all the better.

Your PR portfolio should be viewed as a high impact showcase for your achievements, abilities, skills, and credentials.

This a field with a lot of quality competition.

As you begin your job search, you will need to create and maintain an employer-ready portfolio that introduces you the right way to the right people. Right?

Two Portfolios.

Today, young PR majors will need two portfolios – both a hard-copy version in a binder and an online version.

1. **The Binder Version.** A simple black binder works well. A clean half-inch or one-inch binder with page protectors is a good idea. If you want to add a bit of branding, that's fine – but remember, a PR portfolio is about your clients, not you.

    And, by the way, *it is not a scrapbook.* It can be strong graphically, but "cute" or "funky" should not apply. The content for individual programs might vary – but your portfolio should be nothing but *professional.*

2. **The Online Version.** This should be posted on an easy-to-access website and also be deliverable on a flash drive or CD. If possible, the CD or flash drive version should be nicely packaged.

    Here's what we should find inside both portfolios:

* **An Executive Summary. Table of Contents. Section Dividers.** The binder version should use traditional section dividers and begin with an Executive Summary and Table of Contents. Each sample should also have a summary - with background/ project context and a brief description of your role. From the beginning, keep it neat.

Samples from some of your better projects may be a part of your portfolio for years. Start with good habits.

- **A Home Page. Clear Navigation. Easy-to-Understand Sections.** Your online portfolio should begin with a clear and easy-to-navigate home page. Each case should begin with an appropriate Executive Summary, with background or project context and a brief description of your role.

  A cautionary note: Online portfolios can accommodate a wider range of materials – all manner of videos, audio from radio shows, and scans of all manner of materials: Memos, research reports, and social media archives. From the beginning, you need to develop good archival habits. Save it all. But don't put it all in your portfolio. Start with good habits.

- **Writing Samples. Organized. Summarized.** People will want to see your writing samples: press releases, alerts, features, newspaper clippings, newsletter articles, flyers, brochures, invitations, posters, etc.

  If they've appeared in print or online, develop a clear and good-looking format. For example, for a newspaper article, include the masthead and date information on top.

  Make it as close to the original as possible – to help the reviewer better understand how the document was actually used. You'll need to get good at scans and photocopies.

  Use full-page printouts in your binder version and easy-to-read PDFs for the online version.

  No byline? PR professionals, unlike journalists, often do not have their name in the byline of materials they've written. If your name is not prominently featured on a piece as the writer, create a brief, neat caption that explains your role in, or contribution to, that piece.

- **Plans you've created. Real clients or class projects.** These are important. They show your ability to work through the strategic and creative process in business. **Two things.** 1. Executive Summary, please. Remember, people are busy. 2. Please remove confidential information.

- **Social Media.** These can be from client work; a professional or personal blog or website; Twitter, Instagram, or Facebook posts from internships; volunteer work; or student groups. Screen grabs are often helpful. Include analytics.

- **Digital, graphic design, video production, etc.** Got graphics? Include samples that demonstrate your graphic design or desktop publishing skills along with the writing – if you have these skills. Similarly, feature broadcast or online video you've produced, directed, or edited. Consider a nicely packaged "Best of" CD with screen grabs and Summary Intros.

- **Reference letters, testimonials, and complimentary emails.** If you don't have them, you might want to ask those qualified to write them: Professors, internship supervisors, and former employers. Overall, these examples highlight positive praise for a job well done. Association memberships, awards, and leadership roles in student groups also qualify. We love that third-party validation.

- • **A "Leave Behind."** Give it a thought. Perhaps something with links to an online version of the portfolio. This can be included with a thank you note.

Some Additional Strategic Advice:

- **Your Archive – Start it Now.** As you create your hard copy portfolio, keep a few samples handy in neat, organized electronic form as well. You never know when a potential employer may want to look at "a few more" writing samples. Have samples that you can quickly email.

- **Design it for a first-rate first impression.** You may be wonderfully pleasant in person, but the at-a-distance impact of a first-rate portfolio should never be underestimated. You will have other opportunities during your interview to share your personality, job history, and an understanding of your prospective employer's business. But the true breadth and depth of your PR production skills — especially your writing — will only come out in that portfolio.

- **Respect the time of those reviewing your work.** Erin Enke, an account supervisor at Fleishman-Hillard New York who supervises internship hiring and evaluates entry-level candidates, advises: *"Think in terms of what the employer needs to know about you and what you've done. They don't need to know that you've written a 40-page paper unless that paper discusses new media or some other emerging trend that the organization is interested in."*

- **It's a Portfolio – Not a Scrapbook!** Avoid funky fonts, clever clip art and other frills.
  Enke adds: *"The differentiation will not be 'Who has the cutest clip art?' It comes down to 'Who has the most to contribute to my company?'"*

- **Finally… is it good enough? Make it better anyway.** The hiring process for PR jobs and internships is highly competitive. Every prospective employer will be reviewing stacks of portfolios. A final observation from Erin Enke: *"The winners will be those whose materials speak directly to their PR experience. I know I won't have to train that person about what public relations is or how to write."*

Research, Consumer Insight & Account Planning.

This section isn't about your Research Portfolio. It's more about to whom you'll be presenting that portfolio.

As the interviewing and hiring process begins, the first thing you need to remember is that much of your audience will not be other researchers.

Certainly, there will be a few, but even with those individuals, much of their concern will be how well you communicate with non-researchers.

Your Next Research Task.

It's going to be a challenge. You need to get to know those who will be interviewing you. Before you meet them.

In the case of many larger firms, most of the people you will work with will not be researchers.

If you're interviewing with a large research-specialty firm, this is much different. In that case, your professors may be able to tell you what to expect.

In the business world, your job, for the most part, will be to develop an accurate understanding of the task at hand – with considerable time and budget constraints – and then provide actionable insights to those who respect the work you performed.

They want to know the research outcome, but don't wish to relive that research! That means, in many ways, you have to translate your own concerns into the concerns of others.

One more thing.

Assume you have one minute to make each point. For reports, one experienced researcher recommends *"keep it 1-2 pages per project. And keep it visual."*

That doesn't mean the backing can't include as many pages as necessary – including stacks of printouts. Companies hire researchers so they don't have to deal with stacks of printouts.

That will be your job – and there is often a lot at stake, so they'll want somebody first rate.

And, of course, if you're dealing with other researchers, they will certainly want to know more – but in a quick orderly way. Remember, they're often busy, too.

A Brief Presentation Format.

Here's a brief format for presenting your research in a longer form. In this case, *"Show the journey – not just the destination."* And keep it as brief as possible.

- **Explain the business problem.** One or two sentences.

- **Describe your approach.** Of all possible methods, why this one? Remember, research takes place in a business context. Budgets are often quite constrained. Your approach should offer the best value as well as accuracy.

- **Present your results.** Be brief, but show enough detail to make it clear that you know what you're talking about.

- **Describe major problems** – tell us how you solved them. *This is a chance to show you are a problem solver!*

- **Describe the impact of your work.** Relate your findings back to the business problem. Did you solve it? If not, what did you learn?

Get to Know Your Target Audience.

We'll finish this short section by repeating our initial advice.

The internal environment of companies looking to hire researchers is often much different than the academic research environment. Find out for yourself what that environment is like – and what the decision-makers are like.

In short, get to know your Target Audience – that's something that almost always delivers better results.

Social Media

SOCIAL MEDIA IS IN FULL BLOOM. Job openings are sprouting everywhere, as companies of all sizes look to create or expand their social media campaigns and capability.

They're looking for people with genuine social media skills.

So here is some portfolio inspiration – seven tips for a social media portfolio. Thanks to Keith Quesenberry and Brian Hernandez for their good advice.

1. **Use the technology.** Where's the QR (Quick Response) code? They're easy to make. They immediately show that you're comfortable with an important piece of social media technology. But, just in case the person doing the hiring doesn't use the technology, make sure there's another way to get at your information.

2. **Show above-average technical ability.** For example, Shopify, an ecommerce platform, said they received the

best résumé ever. A person who really wanted to work in Shopify's marketing department literally built an online store using Shopify. Within the platform, he included his background, experience, etc. For the ecommerce part, you could "buy" an interview with him for "$0.00." Shopify's manager of marketing and media observed: *"We get an infinite amount of résumés here. Yes, he got the job."*

3. **Use Facebook. Really use Facebook.** Hey, everybody uses Facebook. But Henry O'Loughlin took to Facebook to showcase his "Social Résumé," including a video describing how to navigate his résumé on Facebook. Here is his very clear selling proposition: *"I work with mostly small businesses doing social media, so I am demonstrating through this resume all of the tools out there that can be utilized without an ad budget."* O'Loughlin used Facebook's Page feature to showcase his skills, as well as show potential clients what he had to offer.

4. **A tricked-out Video résumé?** Short, clever videos can be an important part of a social media campaign.

Why not demonstrate that skill? Here, Graeme Anthony created a clever complement to the usual job-search materials (i.e., print résumé, cover letter and website) with a fun interactive video. Viewers can click on words linked to an "About Me" section, a portfolio, a "Skills" page, Timeline, and Contact information. This demonstrates relevant technical skills at the same time it does the basic job.

5. **Gather your online networks in one place.** Facebook, Tumblr, Twitter, Instagram, Pinterest... that's just the beginning. Another reason companies need social media expertise is they need someone to help keep track of this constantly moving target. Showing that you're in touch with ALL OF IT, is a key hiring criterion.

An example – Alisha Miranda used Flavors.me as an online hub for all of her social media networks. Her profile is essentially an abridged online résumé. In this case, her eventual employer – also social media savvy – monitored her activities for about three weeks to see what she was doing on Tumblr, Twitter, etc. to evaluate her marketing effectiveness and to see if her style matched what was required. Tracy Brisson CEO of The Opportunities Project, the person who hired her and did the monitoring, noted: *"Once I saw that she had all the goods, only then did I contact her to talk. As a career coach and recruiter, I can't emphasize the importance of creating something clients and employers want, which is results and evidence."* You can employ sites like Flavors.me or About.me to showcase all of the social media websites you use. Your existing website or blog are also good spots to place your social media icons.

6. A Print Résumé with contemporary personality.
Here's an example of making a portfolio fit the job you're looking for. This résumé would not put you in "The Hiring Line" for account management, research, or even copywriting. But for social media – yeah, it works. Hey, even the Hamster thing. It reflects her personality and demonstrates that – in social media – you can see what you're getting. In social media, where your personal interface is more important, something like this can work. By the way, in addition to personality, it shows hard work and a certain level of design skill.

7. **The Electronic Pitch Page.** The world of job hunting is a moving target – particularly in social media. There's a company called Beyond Credentials that believes "finding talent based solely on a résumé is fundamentally flawed." Their service helps users build "personalized pitch pages" that list everything you'd have on a print résumé – your "story," accomplishments, a Q&A, and writing samples. The page also includes icons linking to LinkedIn, Facebook, and Twitter profiles. It's all changing. Stay alert!

8. **Social Media. The Power of Third-Party Validation.** When you hear it from a friend, or media you like, or a social media site you trust, that recommendation has power. Your social media portfolio could also benefit from solid third-party endorsements, testimonials, and recommendations. Don't fill your portfolio with just what you say about yourself. If you can have others say it, you unleash the power of the third party. Party on! See some of these examples in more detail on Mashable's site. Here's the link: http://mashable.com/2011/05/20/social-media-resumes/#wEch9xtljiqa
Find out more in Keith Quesenberry's, *Social Media Strategy: Marketing and Advertising in the Consumer Revolution*

Sports Marketing

The sports marketing playing field includes all the major areas of MarCom: Ads, PR, Promotion, Cause Marketing, Database and Direct, New Media, Events, Engagement, and a lot more.

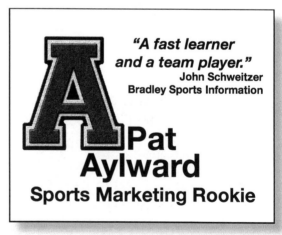

"A fast learner and a team player."
John Schweitzer
Bradley Sports Information

Pat Aylward
Sports Marketing Rookie

Some of the most active and most visited sites are those for major sports teams.

You can now find introductory sports marketing courses at many schools. Try to track down the ones at your school – they may be in a non-traditional part of the program.

Sometimes they're in the Journalism or MassComm department, sometimes in the B school, and sometimes in the Education Department – as part of Physical Education.

As for your sports marketing portfolio, in this field it's often based on apprenticeship in various areas – ticket sales, ad sales for the program, helping with press conference logistics, Sports Information services, and the various websites for your school's different sports teams.

It also wouldn't hurt to try your hand at sports writing for the school newspaper. Sports Information might even let you try your hand at a press release – for the fencing team.

Do Some Scouting.

Just as many pro sports work with minor leagues, the sports marketing career path often involves entering through the internship door. During the summer, many teams have internship slots – baseball, in particular – since that's their busiest time.

If your school has a sports marketing course, take it.

If you can't get in, knock on the instructor's door and ask him or her what books and periodicals you should look at.

There's a Sports Marketing Association. Your school's sports marketing instructor might belong to it already – they have a student membership that's very affordable.

Your School Has a Sports Marketing Training Program.
It's the Athletic Department at your school. Think about it.

They already have a training program in place.

Every year, slots open up in their Sports Information section. Better yet, there's almost always a lot to do.

Almost all the things that a major or minor league sports marketer does – your school does – maybe more.

Go to the Athletic Department. Walk in. That's right, just show up on their doorstep and ask how to get involved.

Either they'll find something for you to do almost immediately – or, if there are already a number of students standing in line, they'll tell you what to do – or how long the wait is.

In sports marketing, athletic departments and university sports information programs literally give you a chance to play your way into a nice portfolio with a chance at some solid accomplishments on your résumé.

Startups

Portfolios can play an important part in helping startups get up and running. Perhaps you'll play an important part as well.

We talked earlier in this book about how your brain is literally changing – reprioritizing, reorganizing, and integrating all kinds of new information. You're entering a new world.

When you think about it, maybe that explains why a lot of bright young people your age discovered that this was the time to get something started.

You've heard the stories. Facebook and Zuckerberg. Bill Gates and his college friends starting Microsoft. This is the time when those ideas start to pop up.

You're entering a whole different world, with a whole different set of objectives and resources. Instead of a job, you're looking for funding – or a partner.

Instead of HR directors, you're looking for VC's, "Angels," incubators, and seed money.

The good news. There's probably never been a better time to give it a try. We're all aware of the success stories, and now there's a whole infrastructure of people who want a piece of "the next big thing." Better yet, you live in the best country on the planet to get a startup started.

The bad news. Hey, not every good idea makes it over the finish line – even the good ones. And it's not uncommon for that "overnight success" to take a few decades.

Many of the same portfolio principles we've been discussing throughout this book apply. And getting involved in one at this stage of your life can be a tremendous learning experience.

It's not your idea? So what? Think of all you're going to learn. And maybe you'll get a small share.

Startups have brand characteristics. You'll find that a lot of what we've been talking about in "Brand You!" applies.

You'll have all the trappings: a URL, a logo, a strategy, a portfolio presentation (online and hard copy), and a quick "elevator pitch." And, by now, you know that short and to-the-point are necessities for success.

As you move through this stage of your education, it's not unusual to run into these startups.

They can take up a ton of your time and attention – and, as you already know, the vast majority don't make it.

But the lessons you learn can end up being a valuable part of your education. It can be a great way to start! Only now, instead of a portfolio, you need an "elevator pitch."

Six Tips for an "Elevator Pitch."

How do you come up with an "elevator pitch?" These six questions can be a good place to start. Try it. It can be fun.

Round up a group of your friends and/or family members who know you well, and try to tell them what you're thinking. Then have them help you answer the questions.

Serve refreshments. Have enough to keep everyone refreshed and nourished. Plan on two hours or so.

1. **What are you?** Describe your business in simple human terms. No jargon, no "consultant speak."

2. **Who is your target**? Be realistic. Describe that target customer. Again, are you being realistic?

3. **Why would this customer use you?** What are your advantages? Is there more than one? Think of all of the reasons. List as many as possible. Then, focus back. What are the one or two main reasons?

4. **What are your competitors' advantages?** Be honest, brutal, and factual. Why are you better? You should have four or five clear, unique selling points/competitive advantages.

5. **What's your brand personality?** Pass around a few recent magazines (travel, music, gossip, home, food, photography, sport). Ask each person there to find one picture that seems to fit the personality of your company. Ask people to present their pictures and the words that describe them. Narrow those words down to four that do the best job of describing your brand.

6. **What's your tone of voice?** Once you have agreed on brand personality keywords, select some supporting words.

The Pitch: Once you've spent time with these basics, you can build your pitch. The format goes something like this:

For _____ (target customers),

who have _____ (customer need),

_____ (company or product name)

is the _____ (market or category name)

that _____ (key benefit).

Unlike _____ (competitive product or service),

our product _____

(point of difference).

Things To Do:

OK, there's a lot here. Let's see if we can move things forward.

Elevator Pitch sentence structure:

FOR (target customer), WHO HAS (customer need), (product name) IS A (market category) THAT (one key benefit). UNLIKE (competition), THE PRODUCT (unique differentiator).

1. **What Category?** So, do you have a career target area yet? If so, make a "wish list" of what you'd like to have in your portfolio. No choice yet? Well, at least you know that.

2. **How's your "OP?"** You've already made some progress, right? What's next on your "To Do" list? Do that.

3. **Start your "Advisory Board."** As you work to develop your portfolio, you'll want a few people you can talk to. You're best off having a few who are already familiar with what you're doing. Buy them a beverage – probably coffee – and tell them what your plans are. Get them involved.

28. Putting Together Your First Portfolio.

HEY, I DIDN'T GET IT RIGHT UNTIL MY THIRD TRY.
When you're still in school, you're still learning. (Actually, you're going to have to keep learning, but you'll learn that soon enough as well.)

The big problem is that we don't yet know what the industry standard is. And, just to make it interesting, we usually don't know what we don't know.

So here's what to do.

Tip #1.
Study Other Portfolios.

Study those in your chosen field – if you can find any – and study others.

Creative portfolios can give you some great ideas.

Go to portfolio school

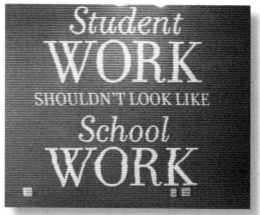

sites and see what's being done. As the Chicago Portfolio School says, *"Student work shouldn't look like school work."*

Try to make sure you're looking at portfolios that were good enough to get job offers.

When I saw a sample portfolio from one of the new courses being offered in New York, that's when the light bulb went on.

Once you know the standard, it's so much easier.

Because now you know what you're aiming at.

Tip#2. Learn About Your Industry.

Learn as much about your industry as you can. Magazines. Web sites. Old postings. Industry gossip.

At first, for all of us, it's kind of a big *"I don't get this. I don't know the names. I'm not even sure what they do."*

But you start to get it. It's another reason that you should be studying up your junior year. It takes a while. And don't just learn about the companies, *learn about the people.*

While I was still going to school, a new ad book came out, *The Copywriter,* by John Matthews, a top Leo Burnett Creative. I read it – and liked it. I wrote him a letter. He answered it.

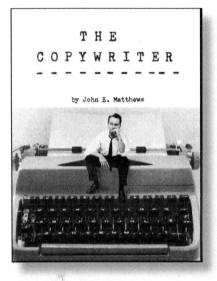

I met John when I went to Chicago for interviews. A year later, with a much better portfolio, he offered me a job.

I didn't take the job, but we stayed in touch. By the time I got to Burnett, he was gone – wealthy and retired.

Some years after that, when I was publishing books and he was moving down to Florida, he sent me his leftover copies. It's still a nice book. Want one?

Remember what I said about being interesting? It even works for big-time executives. Be interested in who they are and what they do. One way or another, it'll help.

Tip #3. Get Feedback. Make It Better.

Naturally, we like it better when people tell us how wonderful we are. But the really valuable stuff is useful criticism.

A qualification – it has to be useful. That *"I don't know, I just don't like it"* stuff may be sincere – but it's not helpful.

Look for those who can offer constructive comments.

One of my first bosses, Bill Ross at JWT, was wonderful at that. You brought in the copy and before he was done – even though he hadn't approved a single word – you could hardly wait to go back to your office and work on the new thing he had just inspired you to do!

Sure, there aren't a lot of people like that, but maybe we don't always look as hard for that next version as we could.

It'll be more work. Gosh, isn't what I did good enough?

A few chapters ago, I suggested forming an Advisory Board. Their opinion on those early drafts of your portfolio could really start to come in handy. Get feedback. Use it.

Tip #4. Invent the Ideal Portfolio.

The basic outline of what you want to do is simple:

How do you make it special?

Here are some thoughts – designed to help you have some thoughts. (I'm trying to be like Bill Ross, and have you rush out to act on that even better idea that I just inspired in your growing and active young mind.)

Some thoughts like…

Really cool packaging – something that represents your industry. If you want to go into sports marketing, how about making up a team logo for yourself. The portfolio? You'll make that like a sporting team press kit. Right?

Going into media? Look at some media sales kits.

Tired of the same old resume? How about a newsletter in the style of your target industry?

Looking for work in events and experiential, or maybe promotion and publicity? Where is that campus event you created and implemented?

Make sure your portfolio presentation comes with lots of "bells and whistles?" You know, posters, T-shirts, photos of the event, and that nice shot of you presenting the big blow-up check to the designated charity.

How about some simple animation on your web site?
Make a Wish list. Make some of it come true.

And, speaking of websites, what are you doing to make it cool? Better yet, make it something I want to navigate –without you at my side explaining it!

Tip #5. Present Your Case Histories Backward.

We mentioned this earlier, but it's worth repeating.

Begin with the conclusion and recommendation.

Present that conclusion in a clear and provocative way. Then, follow up with more information – usually in the form of an Executive Summary, which can quickly state the problem, and how you solved it.

Finally, with proper indexing and navigation cues, you can lead the reader into the whole case. Though it wouldn't hurt to provide a bit more presentation – such as select quotes or video from a focus group or consumer interview.

Tip #6. If you have to explain, think again.

What do you need to explain? Is that how you want to spend your valuable time with this person? First impressions…

Keep the blah-blah to a minimum.

Should you add project or Brief Notes? Use your head. If you're looking for a job as an account exec, project manager, or account planner, of course you should have these things.

In fact, they should be things that you lead with – using an appropriate Summary Intro, of course. Then again, if you're an art director, designer, or copywriter, keep it to a sentence – if that. If there is something in addition that might be of interest, stick it in the back of that particular project.

Well-written project descriptions that allow employers to understand the brief and constraints are important, if it's related to your skills and whether or not someone would hire you.

But remember, even though many things are true, they don't all have to be in your portfolio.

Things To Do:

OK, time to get moving.

❏ **Take a look at web sites featuring student portfolios.** Here are a few. Go find more:

- **FindSpark.** A community dedicated to yoru career success. https://www.findspark.com/creative-online-portfolios-students-recent-grads/

- **Miami Ad School.** Not just creative – also Account Planning and Social Media. http://www.miamiadschool.com/student-work

- **The Student Ad Portfolio is Broken.** This is a provocative discussion posted by Digiday. http://digiday.com/agencies/pulsepointes-ad-portfolio-broken/

- **SEO Winner!** This Canadian advertising/design student managed to get her excellent portfolio up to the top of the Google search engine. https://issuu.com/miss.design/docs/victoria.k.book-11x14_portrait?e=1221191/5255470

- **American Marketing Association.** They have an "Ask the Expert" piece on putting a portfolio together – kind of generic. https://archive.ama.org/archive/Careers/Pages/C2C%20Ask%20the%20Expert/C2C_Ask_the_Expert_Putting_a_Portfolio_Together.aspx

- **How to Create a Killer Marketing Portfolio.** Great headline. Generic advice. http://www.everydayinterviewtips.com/how-to-create-a-killer-marketing-portfolio/

- **Public Relations Portfolios. Here are 10 Things Every PR Portfolio Must Have.** A good starting point. http://www.prdaily.com/Main/Articles/10_things_every_PR_portfolio_must_have_14103.aspx

- **Fashion Marketing.** When you do your Google search, be sure to add modifiers to the phrase student portfolio. Here's some nice advice on fashion marketing. http://searchingfor-style.com/2016/01/10-elements-fashion-business-market-ing-portfolio/

- **Social Media.** Why you should have a portfolio if you work in social media. This is from an industry group. You need to reach out to get all the information you can. http://wersm.com/why-you-should-have-a-portfolio-if-you-work-in-social-media/

❏ **Learn About the Industry you want to work in.**

- **Subscribe.** Find a way to read about the industry. If it's advertising, your school library should be getting *Ad Age* and *AdWeek* at the student rate. If not, talk to your instructor. Other industries – find out what to read.

- **Search.** There's plenty online – industry groups and leading firms. Track 'em down and spend some time.

- **Visit.** Find the nearest major players in your target industry – schedule an informational visit. Need a reason? Make it a school project. Or "Independent Study." Bring a camera and/or video. Do a report – present it on PowerPoint.

❏ **Learn About the People.** Nationally and locally. Who are they. What do they do? What do they think? Many have speeches available. Or books. Find them. Read them.

- **Read All About It.** Find a book. Or a speech. Read it. Write the person who wrote it with an intelligent question.

❏ **Form Your Feedback Team.** Then, book a meeting – either with all of them, or each of them. In person is best of all (you pay for the beverage of choice) with real work to evaluate and talk about.

❏ **Write down some thoughts about your Ideal Portfolio.** Read about other portfolios. Imagine what yours could be.

❏ **Got a Case History?** See if you can build it backward.

❏ **Eliminate Explanations.** Anything need explaining in your portfolio? How can you get rid of it? How can you design your communications so that it's not needed?

29. The Road Ahead...

THE TRAIL YOU LEAVE BEHIND is just one of the things you'll keep running into as you travel The Road Ahead.

Keep that in mind as you make your way on your chosen career path – or the one that chooses you.

These days, we all leave a digital trail, so mind your "O.P."

Before you send out that snarky e-mail – the one that really tells that person what you think – let it sit for one day more.

You can't UnSend – and life doesn't have a Rewind button. That said, don't let that stop you from hitting Play and really enjoying the heck out of the 21st Century.

But go easy on that Fast Forward.

There's a lot out there waiting for you. The digital revolution has created an absolute explosion of art, music, and literature. It's full of film, video, theater, and what the media and marketing folks like to call "content." Enjoy it.

The most deprived person in our country has more media and information available to them at low or no cost than the crowned heads of Europe had just one hundred years ago.

This is no small matter.

The materials available to "feed" that non-linear processing tool between our ears – the human brain – is here in abundance. Take advantage. Enjoy the feast.

What do we want to know? What do we want to think about? What do we want to do? It's out there and – all things considered – it's pretty easy to access.

What You Have to Do. vs. What You Want to Do.

As for making a living, you really do have some options – some pretty important ones. And I'm going to suggest one more that just might enrich your life.

245

Do a few things for their own sake. I'm fairly certain that you'll find enough things to do that you'll get paid for.

Well and good. But as you move on that Road Ahead, you just might find some other things that you want to do simply because... well, because you want to. Do them.

It may be a family and children – it may be a cause that you believe in – it may be a project that you and a few friends feel like starting up. Go for it.

Or, as Dan Wieden said, *"just do it."*

I've had a tremendously satisfying career. It let me learn a lot of useful things – and then I was able to use that knowledge on behalf of those I want to help.

And that's helped me do things I want to do.

I don't get paid for a lot of that stuff. And I don't care. The pay-off in lifetime satisfaction will do just fine, thank you.

I did lots of ads, back in the day, had a great time, won my share of awards – but I still get greater satisfaction from the people I helped than I do from all that shiny stuff now getting dusty on the shelf.

So, as you make your way in the world doing the best you can – and, hopefully, doing it well – don't miss out on the opportunity to do even more – just because you want to.

And I hope you discover this wonderful truth...

"When you enjoy what you do,
you'll never work a day."

Good luck to you.

Give your gift.

Appendix A:
The Personal Brand Matrix.

WE ADDED THIS SECTION after we printed up the initial edition. We'd like to thank Frank Blossom of Grand Valley State and The Polishing Center.

Frank
@ Polishing Center

Frank's an early adopter of our books, a contributor to some of our projects, and someone who uses our techniques and tactics to good success – for his students.

They've been using 3-Ups as part of their portfolio development for a number of years. In fact, Frank has developed some effective tactics based on the 3-Up. Like this one...

Three Kinds of 3-Ups.

First, his students do three kinds of 3-Ups.

1. **The Original** – Blank, good for thank you notes and lists

2. **The Mini-Résumé** – A short edited version.

3. **Your Brand Story** – the limited space on a 3-Up does a nice job of enforcing editing discipline. Students write a short narrative of who they are and what they want to accomplish.

So far, so good.

Frank has actually had students get jobs just with those three kinds of 3-ups. He observed that those hiring were impressed to receive three consistent branded messages.

After reviewing the Preview Edition of Brand You, he wrote me a note – with an important improvement. This one.

His students use The MarCom Matrix as a framework for developing their own personal brand. Hmm... interesting.

There's a MarCom Matrix Worksheet back on page 71. Stripped down, it kind of looks like this.

This framework puts the major MarCom disciplines on one page, with the Brand or Idea at the center.

We covered those various disciplines in Chapter 12. Putting them together in the Matrix helps you to think of

THE MARCOM MATRIX:
• Advertising • Public Relations
• Direct Response • Sales Promotion
Database & CRM • Events & Experiential
• New Media / Interactive

and visualize the range of possibilities and inter-connections.

Often, whatever discipline we work in will tend to dominate. Ad people think in of solving the problem with an ad campaign, PR people will think of a PR solution. Database marketers look for a database. And so on.

As the saying goes, *"When all you have is a hammer, every problem looks like a nail."* The MarCom Matrix moves us all toward a more holistic "Swiss Army Knife" approach.

That worksheet on page 71 can help. Grab it on our adbuzz website. Look in Café. http://www.adbuzz.com/resources/ CWW4_MatrixWorksheet.pdf

To get your heads set for your personal brand, let's cover the MarCom disciplines once more. We already did it once in Chapter 12 but let's do it again. A bit of repetition never hurt.

Chances are, you're very familiar with some, and don't give others much thought.

The ones you don't use much, think of them as blades on your Swiss Army Knife that still need a bit of development – and sharpening.

Advertising

Simply put, advertising involves messages in paid media. Since you're paying for it, you have quite a bit of control.

That said, what do you want to say? How little can you pay? Remember, a lot of things that look like ads – brochures, posters, and "sample" ads – might look terrific in your portfolio without your actually having to pay for them.

You might also see if there isn't some local client you can "adopt." A classic of this kind of thing is Elmer's Minnows – a small bait shop in Minnesota that was "adopted" by the legendary copywriter Tom McElligott early in his career.

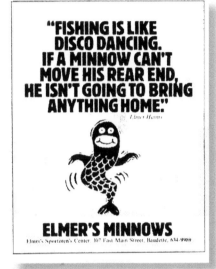

"FISHING IS LIKE DISCO DANCING. IF A MINNOW CAN'T MOVE HIS REAR END, HE ISN'T GOING TO BRING ANYTHING HOME."

ELMER'S MINNOWS

After Tom did some terrific little ads – like this one – they were still a small bait shop – but Tom had award-winning ads in his portfolio.

Public Relations

If you're not experienced in PR, here are a few initial thoughts (If you're already experienced, you should already know this.)

1. Your initial audience is often the media "gatekeeper." Think of what you can say that would be interesting for that medium. If you have an interesting photo, that's even better.

2. Make it interesting to the media's audience. Work to see things through the eyes of the audience.

3. Third Party Technique/Third Party Endorsement. When someone else says something nice, it's more effective

– whether it's a movie or restaurant review, or someone who said something nice about you. Hold that thought. The "Third Party Effect" is still a powerful tool.

Remember, it's not who you know, it's who knows you.

Direct Marketing, Database, and CRM.

Google, the internet, your computer, and a whole range of database and sales management programs have made these activites more do-able for all of us.

Starting with a personal database, learn to think like a direct marketer as you expand your relationships, your connections, and your knowledge of the marketplace. We covered this in Chapters 15, 17, 19, and 20. Forgot? Read 'em again.

Today, it's easier-than-ever to make connections.

This is a good thing.

Sales Promotion.

Simply put, sales promotion involves the use of some kind of incentive to stimulate the desired behavior.

Win/Free/Save is the simple summary of the incentives used, though in the case of "Cause Marketing," that incentive might be attached to a worthy cause.

Another view of it, used by Larry Minsky, one of my own personal favorite sales promo gurus (Colleen, you're my other favorite) is *"What's the bribe?"* A bit crass, perhaps, but it forces you to think about what it's really going to take to get the behavioral result you're looking for.

Events and Experiential.

If you're a student, you're usually swimming through this kind of marketing – from the sign-up tables during Freshman Week, to the related activities at concerts and games, to that full-blown Experience Fest known as Spring Break.

New Media/Interactive.

This single category actually encompasses all of the MarCom channels – each in its own unique way.

It's a delivery channel for advertising. Including search.

It's a channel and a forum for public relations.

It can be a unique – and very effective – direct/database collection and distribution platform.

It can be a delivery system for sales promotion incentives and a source of sales promotion incentives in its own right.

For example, the 'Net can deliver a sweepstakes entry, a music download, or a coupon delivered to your e-mail address That's "Win/Free/Save!"

As for Cause Marketing, think Ice Bucket Challenge – an online event that went "viral."

It raised a whopping $220 million. (Better yet, there are already some ALS treatment improvements generated by research activities funded by the Challenge.) Got a cause?

Good for you!

Your Personal Branding Framework.

OK, let's modify the MarCom Matrix to focus on your own lesser-known, smaller budget personal brand – still in development.

Ready... Fire... AIM!

Sometimes we earn by doing it first. Then, if we don't quite hit the mark, we do it again – with better aim and performance.

We're smarter. Practice makes perfect.

As you develop your personal brand, this may happen more than once. We talked about this in Chapter 11 - Getting Better.

Here's a MarCom Matrix for our own Personal Brand.

We made some important changes to the various categories. We changed Advertising and Public Relations into this…
Advertising & Public Relations = Message Windows.
Direct Response, Database, and CRM was turned into…
Direct Marketing and Your Personal Database.
Sales Promotion, Events, and Experiential were combined into **Parties & Presents.** Sound like fun? You bet.

Then, New Media/Interactive turns into **Your "O.P." Your Online Presence.** That was part of Chapter 15, but now it will be a more integrated part of your whole Personal Brand Plan. Ready? Let's go!

Advertising & Public Relations = Message Windows.

You need to look for opportunities for your brand. First, let's be clear about what we mean by "Message Windows."

If your cat ran away and you needed to put up some signs, your "message windows" would be the trees and phone poles a block or two from your house. Right?

When we say the "M" word (Media), it often forces us into thinking about buying our message space. Not necessarily.

Yes, you may have to purchase media– assuming it's worth it. But you also have to think of other "windows of opportunity."

For example, a cool T-shirt design, or a poster you can put up (legally) somewhere on campus – like the door of your dorm room. Hey, it's a start – and it still goes in your portfolio.

That design on your 3-Up – will it go anywhere else?

Let's see what else you can do for your personal brand.

Advertising Opportunities.

There may actually be some advertising opportunities – how about an inexpensive program ad? Sure, a prospective employer won't see the program, but he'll see the ad in your portfolio.

Even though, for the most part, ordinary paid media ads aren't usually available to individuals just starting out, there still may be a unique opportunity for a poster or some other piece of OOH (Out of Home). Poster. T-shirt. Yard sign.

We all have to start somewhere. And, whether or not those first small advertising efforts have big-time results, you're starting to acquire valuable experience.

And, there may be actual media opportunities – ads for a local newspaper or radio station – a poster idea for a party or concert – even a T-shirt. What about an ad in the campus newspaper? Or the campus radio station? Bus bench back?

Public Relations Opportunities.

Got something to say? Say it. Put the reprint in your portfolio.

An article you wrote – a short funny poem about a campus event (just right to fill a bit of space in the campus newspaper), a letter to the editor – a book or movie review.

See what you can do to "get some press," and, remember, your first audience is the media "gatekeeper" the person who decides what gets used. Write with that "gatekeeper" in mind, as well as the ultimate audience. Make their job easier.

And, again, got something to say? Say it!

Volunteer Opportunities.

There may be an organization, a worthy cause, a local business, or even a local politician, who needs some help – go for it.

Doing *"pro bono"* work – for free –can generate valuable samples, valuable connections and valuable experience.

As I mentioned, my volunteer work for local politicians led to – years later – bigger projects.

Better yet, I had fun, made friends, and learned about a whole other side of the communication industry.

Direct Marketing and Your Personal Database
[Direct Response, Database, and CRM]

Developing your Personal Brand in this area will involve two related tasks:

1. **Building Your Database**

2. **Using Your Database.**

We covered this in Chapters 15, 17, 19 and 20. Now's the time to really start to put this into action.

For the Building Your Database part, start with people you know – friends, relatives, family friends and maybe a few school connections. Then, start developing a career focus.

Want to be in Sports Marketing? Connect with the people in your school's sports information department, and, soon thereafter, executives in every minor league and major league sports team you can track down.

Start to grow our database in the direction you think you want your career to go. Ready? Aim… Fire off a 3-up.

And that's the second thing – Using Your Database – don't just let it sit there. For example, why not develop some sort of Contact Info card you can send? Design it. Send it. Fire!

Your 3-Up is a good way to start. Turn it into a postcard.

Send it so people know how to reach you during summer vacation. Or, get a branded envelope together and send it out that way – with a nice stamp on it.

Maybe you'll include a copy of a favorite cartoon – or an article that you think is kind of cool – or an update of how you and your Brand are doing. Or something about your summer job – or the trip you're going to take. Whatever.

Make it appropriate for the audience.

Start with your 3-Up – and then maybe something extra.

OK – now it's time to have a bit of fun with your brand.

Parties & Presents
[Sales Promotion, Events, and Experiential]

That's right, Parties and Presents. You can see why we think this part of personal your brand-building can be a lot of fun.

Let's start with the presents - your first crack at Sales Promotion - an incentive for people to think you're kinda cool.

Presents. Think. What affordable item represents you and your brand? In the beginning, I'd give *Kind of Blue,* the best-selling jazz album of all time.

Check it out if you've never heard it - you can even study to it. Anyway, once you select something, find out where you can get the best price.

You want something that reinforces an aspect of your "brand." There might be a book that you think is worth sharing.

After I published my own books and a CD of songs I'd written and produced, it got a lot easier – sort of. But finding gift-size items that fit your "brand" is something everyone can do.

Find things that are a fit with your brand and who you are.

Those things become your "signature items." Lorelei and I have been giving a delicious coffee cake – a Kringle – as part of our holiday tradition. Have some gift traditions that are part of your "brand." Give it a thought.

Parties. This is going to be fun. We all need to be, as they say, *"the party that knows how to throw one."*

Lorelei likes the Oscars and all three Triple Crown races.

For fiteen years, my sister had the Wren Circle Mother's Day Brunch. Her friends brought their mothers. Roger (her husband) and a few other guys were the waiters. There was a logo on the invitations – and the aprons.

One year it was on Phoenix TV.

You can blame me for hosting the April Fool Film Festival in Chicago. People brought awful commercials.

We had fun and the posters – like the one on the right – won awards, though the commercials didn't.

So it seems to me that your brand should have at least one annual event – a party. It should have: a name, a cool logo, some sort of item – T-shirt, poster, apron, whatever… and, over time, that "Event" will become a part of your brand. Better yet, we'll have a good time.

Your "O.P." Your Online Presence
[New Media/Interactive]

Look for ways to dial up your "O.P." in every MarCom area.

For advertising and PR, find online "Message Windows."

As you become more of a direct marketer, keep expanding your database and find ways to develop richer contacts. (Just saw this article – thought you'd like it. Here's the link.)

Make people aware of things you've done. (Just helped produce this video – here's the link.) Then, do more of them.

And, of course, when you've added something worth experiencing on your website, you could even let us know.

How do I get started?

Frank Blossom gave me some final advice – it's the same advice that he gives to his students:

- Focus on something that's true about you.
- Think about what you like to do.
- Use something people say about you.

One of his students used the metaphor of coffee. Her résumé looked like a coffee container - and she definitely came across as alert and high energy. Caffeinated, to say the least.

She was one of 50 to be invited to an AAF Most Promising Multicultural Students Program in New York. Her unique résumé got 15 interviews – everyone wanted to meet her. Those who met her received a special thank you - her own branded coffee cup - full of beans - with a nice note.

She was hired by a top New York agency, and Frank tells me that she was recently promoted to Creative Director.

So think of that as a Wake-Up call. Let's get going!

Things to Do:

Let's summarize with a few bullet points – and then, you should start making it real.

1. **Advertising.**

- **Find some easy-to-open "windows."** Look for local media channels that offer message windows.

- **OOH Yes!** Is there a location that needs a cool poster?

- **And...** are there any other opportunities for your brand?

- **Volunteer!** Have your brand give a helping hand. Who could use some help? Is there something special you can add ? An ad? A poster? A commemorative coffee cup? If it's a charity or non-profit, you might be able to get free ad space.

- **Get Out the Vote!** Are there any local political races – and deserving candidates – that need a helping hand? Show up.

2. Public Relations.

- **Articles, Reviews, Letters to the Editor.** This can be a good way to start. After they're printed, save them.

- **Cause Marketing.** As we said, we live in a world that could use a bit of help – what can you do? Are there any publicity opportunities? Help make it happen.

- **Politics.** Ditto. Plus you get some nice opportunities to learn and to connect.)Still have friends from those days.)

- **Sports.** Every local team has ongoing needs. And there are never enough cool slogans on T-shirts. But skip the tattoo.

3. Direct Marketing and Your Personal Database.

- **Notify.** Create a postcard size version of your 3-up with current contact info. Do a "summer vacation version."

- **Design a branded envelope** – figure out how to print them on your printer. Get cool stamps. (www.usps.com)

- **Send stuff.** Birthday greetings. Announcements. Congrats.

- **Create a newsletter.** Make it one that can be sent by e-mail and real mail (a PDF will do it). Start by planning one for the end of your school year – share your summer plans and your "next step" career plans. Make sure it includes some brand ID and a nice picture of you.

- **And so on...** Think of other enclosures that fit your "brand" – a cartoon, an article, a copy of a poster you helped create – maybe something that pertains to your hoped-for career.

4. Presents and Parties.

- **Make a list:** Gifts you'd like to give that represent you – Music, books, T-shirts with a logo, tasty food items.

- **Suppliers.** Look at some promotional items catalogs and websites. Take a look at what they offer.

- **Design a coffee cup.**

- **Create a poster** for your branded event – doesn't matter whether or not it exists. Add it to your portfolio.

- **Make a list:** Possible parties – Date/Place/Reason – think about making one of them happen.

- **Name Your Party.** Sketch out an initial logo. What should it go on? Poster. Hat.

5. Your "O.P." Your Online Presence.

- **LinkedIn.** Look at your LinkedIn profile – look for ways to make it a bit better. How's the photo?

- **Facebook.** Post something on Facebook.
  – **"TBT."** Celebrate Throwback Thursday with a blast from your past – like a favorite bit of music on YouTube.
  – **Share.** Share a link to something worth sharing.

- **Google yourself.** What's going on? Who are you? Set some Online Awareness Objectives.

- **Tweet!** #BrandYou – if you're Tweeting, set some goals and topic areas.

Personal Brand MarCom Plan:

Here's a basic worksheet: Fill in those blanks!

Advertising.

- _____
- _____
- _____

Public Relations.

- _____
- _____
- _____

Direct Marketing and Your Personal Database

- _____
- _____
- _____

Presents and Parties

- _____
- _____
- _____
- _____

Your "O.P." Your Online Presence

- _____
- _____
- _____

About the Author:

SO WHAT DID BRUCE DO? He went into the advertising business, at the tail end of the *Mad Men* era, with offers from Chicago's three biggest ad agencies.

He started at JWT/Chicago and was lucky enough to be part of creative groups that came up with the UnCola and DieHard campaigns. He didn't do these ads, but they still make him smile. As he likes to say, he was *"in the room when they happened."*

The DieHard fights
the common cold

He became a Copy Group Head in just two years. Then, moved to a boutique where he won top awards working with Dave Kennedy, (later, of Wieden + Kennedy, the Nike agency).

In his spare time, Bruce helped local political campaigns and his favorite local rock band.

Then he went to Leo Burnett and became their youngest-ever vp/Creative Director, working on clients like P&G. Next, he started a creative consulting practice, and a music production company with that rock band. His clients included Apple Computer, Coors, a President of the United States, Popeyes Fried Chicken, the Washington Post and a lot of other stuff.

One year, he and wife, Lorelei, produced 104 TV commercials – all in one year – that's a lot.

Too much, actually.

Bruce's advice for creatives: *"marry your producer."*

Around that time, he wrote *The Copy Workshop Workbook* – one of the very first books to be developed on Apple's new desktop publishing platform (Lorelei produced that, too).

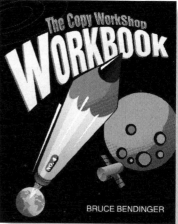

The book grew into a small publishing company – The Copy Workshop – which features some of the more useful books in advertising and marketing: *"best practices in a reader-friendly format."*

Another imprint – First Flight Books – is dedicated to helping first-time authors. And poets.

FIRST FLIGHT BOOKS

Bruce has done a few other things as well. His documentary, *Accidental Army: The Amazing True Story of the Czechoslovak Legion*, is helping a small nation recover its own revolutionary heritage. Ken Burns called it: *"A noble undertaking: A history lost, returned to its people and the world."*

Bruce's CD, *Can't Sing. Don't Care. Songs from the Hip* is available for anyone with fairly low musical standards. We're

pretty sure Amazon has plenty

If you'd rather read books, we recommend *The Book of Gossage,* regarded as one of the "Ten Best" advertising books. We agree.

It's also available on Amazon. Bruce helped write that one, too.

Talent runs in the family. His daughter, Jessica, wrote the hit movie, *Bring It On,* and wrote and directed *Stick It!* She says she's thinking about other movies with the word "it" in the title. Here's a *Bring It On* premiere photo.

As for the rest, we think Google will do a pretty good job telling you more than you want to know.

Early in his career, Bruce says he received a lot of valuable help and good advice from smart, talented people.

With this book, he hopes to return the favor.

We'd also like to thank the smart, talented people who helped transform *Brand You!* from an idea into this rather nice book:

Author/Editor: Bruce Bendinger
Publisher: Lorelei Davis Bendinger
Cover Design: Greg Paus
Proofing/Editorial Assistance: Cari Brookbanks
InDesign Production Assistance: Patrick Aylward
Office Manager: Eugenia Velazquez